"Comedians, through humor, like to get to the heart of the matter. Dr. Sauvage gets to the matter of the heart. A comedian's only goal is to get a laugh. Dr. Sauvage, with his book *The Open Heart,* opens up the mind and the heart of the reader to the magic of love."

—Bob Hope

"*The Open Heart* is an inspiring account of a unique approach to surgical treatment—spiritual as well as physical healing. It is an exciting and uplifting story that can be recommended not only to physicians and medical students but also to anyone yearning for a fulfilled life."

—Michael E. DeBakey, M.D.
Baylor College of Medicine

"Lester Sauvage is that rare individual who has merged the technical, intellectual and spiritual aspects of surgery into a seamless whole. Here he recounts how that unified vision has vivified his own life and the lives of so many fortunate patients."

—C. Rollins Hanlon, M.D., F.A.C.S.
Executive Consultant, American College of Surgeons

"This book would sell as a great collection of stories, or as a classic fairy tale: the poor boy who became a famous surgeon and made discoveries that have saved thousands of lives. To me it is the simple testimony of a man who has found happiness through his devotion to service for others. Lester's deep concern for each of his patients stems from his love of God and his belief that real fulfillment is found only through serving others.

"At a time when cynicism and frustration are overtaking so many in our profession, I count it a privilege and a joy to know Dr. Sauvage and I hope that every surgeon in our land will pause long enough to read his exciting story. Not only will it stimulate us to look to the quality of our service to others, but it will prove to be a prescription for our own happiness."

—Paul W. Brand, M.D.
Author, *Pain: The Gift Nobody Wants*

The Open Heart

Stories of Hope, Healing and Happiness

Lester R. Sauvage, M.D.
and
His Patients

Health Communications, Inc.
Deerfield Beach, Florida

Library of Congress Cataloging-in-Publication Data

Sauvage, Lester R., date
    The open heart : stories of hope, healing, and happiness / Lester
R. Sauvage.
      p. cm.
    ISBN 1-55874-391-X (hardcover). — ISBN 1-55874-383-9
(trade pbk.)
    1. Heart—Surgery—Patients—Biography. 2. Heart—Surgery—
Patients—Religious life. 3. Sauvage, Lester R., date. 4. Heart—
Surgery—Psychological aspects. 5. Self-realization—Religious
aspects. I. Title.
RD598.S28   1996
362.1'97412'00922—dc20
[B]   95-49246
                                         CIP

©1996 Lester R. Sauvage
ISBN 1-55874-383-9 trade paperback
ISBN 1-55874-391-X hardcover

Publisher: Health Communications, Inc.
               3201 S.W. 15th Street
               Deerfield Beach, Florida 33442-8190

Cover design by José Villavicencio; cover illustration by Rita Thomas

Contents

Foreword

Mother Teresa
Missionaries of Charity, Calcutta, India

God has created each one of us for greater things—to love and to be loved. There is no other meaning to our lives than this—loving and being loved—and that is the reason that God commands us to love Him and each other, because He made us for that, and we will not be happy or holy without love.

To satisfy our hunger to be loved by Him, God sent His only Son to show us how much He loves us and to die for us out of love. To satisfy our hunger to love Him, He gives us each other. For every act of love done to my neighbor is done to God Himself; as Jesus said, "Whatever you did to the least of my brothers, you did it to Me."

That is why it is not enough just to do good works—no, our works must be acts of love. In his book, *The Open Heart,* Dr. Lester Sauvage and his patients tell how the practice of medicine can become real love in action—not just curing bodies, but helping people to know the joy of loving, of giving, and of being loved in return. Dr. Sauvage and his patients have discovered that it is not how much we do that matters, but how much love we put in what we do. And our happiness and holiness consist in doing God's will—that is, loving—with a big smile.

My prayer for all who read *The Open Heart* is that each one may keep the joy of loving in his heart and share that joy with others through works of love which are always works of peace. Let us give each other not only our hands to serve, but also our hearts to love with kindness and humility.

Let us pray.

God bless you,

lu Teresa mc.

Prayer

Jesus is Pleased to Come to Us!

As the *TRUTH* to be Told!

And the *LIFE* to be Lived!

As the *LIGHT* to be Lighted!

And the *LOVE* to be Loved!

As the *JOY* to be Given!

And the *PEACE* to be Spread!

Mother Teresa, M.C.

Foreword

C. Everett Koop, M.D., Sc.D.

When Lester Sauvage asked me to write this foreword, it was difficult to follow my usual policy and say no, because Lester is not only an old friend but a remarkable man—and this is a remarkable book! Physicians might occasionally confide to a friend what deep spiritual beliefs motivate their lives, but they seldom write such a frank exposition of their spiritual thoughts, arrived at after long experience and much introspection. But Lester also believes that part of the success he achieved with the difficult heart surgery he performed happened because he helped his patients spiritually as well as physically in the course of their complex care. And indeed this dynamic synergism changed lives.

There is more. It is not only unusual to have a surgeon bare his soul and reveal that he is unashamed to do that with his patients, but this book contains the testimonies of 10 patients who confirm the critical message Dr. Sauvage wants to deliver: happiness and improved total health are to be found by embracing each day to the fullest, by talking to God and listening, too, and by serving God by serving humanity.

Patients and prospective patients will be comforted to know that there are physicians like Lester Sauvage. They might even feel moved to send a copy of this book to their own doctors. After reading it, physicians and other health-care givers of a similar bent to Lester's might be encouraged to be more open with their patients.

This book speaks to my current interest in reforming health care by reforming medical education. Would that this book be required reading for medical students to assist them in becoming the communicating, humanitarian physicians of the 21st century.

In a sense, Lester writes about the same things—from a slightly different perspective—that have been brought to our attention by Norman Cousins and Bernie Siegel. There is a new science in the offing, and we get insights into its future when we learn the effects of attitude, belief, expectation and prayer on patient outcomes.

Written a decade from now, Lester might be talking about psycho-neuro-endocrino-immunology. Whatever the mechanism, Lester Sauvage shows that it works today for doctor and patient alike.

Preface

This book is for people who are seeking increased happiness in their lives and, in addition, desire the benefits that this mental state can bring to their physical health. It is a powerful story of the spiritual impact that doing open-heart surgery for 33 years had on me and what this experience did for thousands of my patients. It tells how life-threatening heart disease and other life crises, the performing and the receiving of open-heart surgery, and the interactions between my patients and me have molded our sense of values and priorities of life, and in doing so have brought greater love and joy into our lives. I invite you to become one with my patients as they journey to the edge of life and then return to health. In these amazing travels I believe that you will discover the same priceless spiritual treasures in your life that they have found in theirs. The raw emotion encountered in these stories has brought my patients and me closer to God, and we believe that it will do the same for you, too.

In the context of our rapidly passing earthly days, this life is a fleeting experience for all of us—so short, so fragile, and yet so precious. In this book, 10 of my patients and I tell you the stories of our lives and hold nothing back. Because I comment after each of their stories, I tell my story first so you can get to know me at the onset and find greater continuity in what I say.

In the second chapter, "Finding the Spirit Within," I tell how I interacted with my patients to help both their physical and spiritual hearts. Through this process I, too, found great joy and continue to do so. After the riveting patient stories, I conclude with the chapter "Following the Spirit Within." In this chapter I bring the lessons that my patients and I have learned in the process of experiencing and treating life-threatening heart disease into the clear focus of a three-step spiritual action plan. This plan is guaranteed to bring increased happiness into our lives as we, together—all of us—continue our journeys to eternity with love overflowing from our open hearts.

Lester R. Sauvage, M.D.

Message to All My Patients

I am grateful from the depths of my spiritual heart to all of you for having entrusted your lives to me. We have inspired each other to be all that we could be by our mutual trust, caring and courage through the crisis days of your surgeries. And our friendship since is a priceless treasure to me. No words that I can say are adequate to express the love that is in my heart for each of you.

This book is really about all of you, though of necessity it has had to focus on only a few of your lives. I thank you, Joe, Julia, Marta, Patsy, Mac, June, Anna, Billy, Chuck and Merilyn, for accepting my invitation to share your lives with our readers and for doing so with enthusiasm. Your message is one of hope and of faith in God and in the wonders of life. It is a call for love and happiness in the spiritual heart of every human being. On behalf of all who may read your words, I thank you from the depth of my soul.

Lester R. Sauvage, M.D.

Message to My Wife and Children

I dedicate this book to you, Mary Ann, my sweetheart, and to our children—Lester Jr., John, Paul, Helen, Joe, Laura, Billy, and Mary Ann—for you, my family, are the inspiration that has made this effort possible. Sweetheart, you are the light of my life, and I love you and each of our children with all my heart and soul. You and the children are a glorious gift from God to me, and I am deeply grateful to you, my dear, for always being available for them and for me.

My children, I am deeply thankful to you for being understanding of my having to be at the hospital during so much of the time while you were growing up. Mother deserves enormous credit for your being the wonderful people you are today as you find joy in your homes and live your lives for God and family.

All my love,
Your husband and father

Acknowledgments

When the future of this book looked bleak in late 1993, Patti Payne, public affairs director for KIRO Radio & Radio House in Seattle, said she believed in it and arranged for my wife and me to meet Mr. Robert Fulghum, the famous author of *All I Need to Know I Learned in Kindergarten* and other best sellers. He was most generous of his time, and after reading my manuscript, said it had much promise but needed the help of his Seattle editor, Phyllis Hatfield. I then worked intensively under Phyllis's direction for the next six months, and this manuscript took definitive shape. Following that productive process I worked for the next year and a half further developing and refining the text, with the aid of critiquing by many people, and this book as you now have it is the result.

Throughout the five years that I worked on this book, my wife was a vital source of advice, direction and inspiration for me. She was also of great help in the patient interviews. Despite her patience, I suspect that she must have occasionally felt like screaming when I would say, for the umpteenth time "Dear, what do you think about this?" or "Would you please read that?"

My manuscript assistants at The Hope Heart Institute— Carol Alto, Austine Goldsmith and Christine Taylor—were loyal supporters, as they transcribed this volume time and time again and recorded the seemingly endless changes. Their frank comments about what I had written were also of great help to me.

I owe great thanks to Duncan Jaenicke, my agent for *The Open Heart,* for his innumerable and invaluable contributions to this project, during which we have also become close friends.

I wish also to express my deepest thanks to my publishers, Peter Vegso and Gary Seidler, and their wonderful staff at Health Communications, Inc. for all they have done to make this book the success that it is. My patients and I are grateful beyond measure for the privilege of working with such fine people.

I wish to express my profound gratitude to Mother Teresa, M.C., and C. Everett Koop, M.D., Sc.D., for the magnificent forewords that they have written for *The Open Heart.* I continue to be deeply moved by Mother Teresa's inspirational words, which provide guidance for all of us.

I wish to give special thanks to Dr. Malay Patel, for speaking with Mother Teresa on my behalf and asking her to read the manuscript of *The Open Heart* and consider lending her support to it. Dr. Patel, a native of India, was a Hope Heart Institute vascular surgery trainee under my direction from 1988-1990, and he is now a vascular surgeon in Ahmedabad, India.

I also wish to express my deepest gratitude to all those who have endorsed this book. To them and all the others who have made this book possible, my patients and I express our deepest appreciation.

My Life

Lester Sauvage, M.D.

I was born at home in the back bedroom of our small, white frame house in a farming community called Wapato, population 1,200, in central Washington state, on November 15, 1926. There were two of us, my sister Coco, who was two and a half years older, and I. Our parents were both of French extraction, which was was not uncommon in that part of the state. The French had come because of the availability of fertile farmland. Our mother, Laura Brouillard, was born in Crookston, Minnesota, and our father, Lester Sauvage, in Durango, Colorado.

Mama was a strong-willed, beautiful woman who never cut her long black hair, which she wore as a thick braid down her back around home, and up on her head in regal style when she went out. She loved hats, especially those with wide and colorful brims, and had a different one for every occasion. She was a forceful person with a commanding presence. Her first husband, a Dr. Cameron, was a respected physician in Yakima, a city of about 18,000 people in central Washington. Mama never spoke of him. Coco learned years later from an aunt, one of Mama's sisters, that he had killed himself a few years after their marriage. No one knew or would say why he did this. They had no children.

A few months after Dr. Cameron's shocking suicide, my flamboyant mother opened a restaurant in Yakima called the Cat and Fiddle. She was a wonderful cook, and people came from far and near. My father, a traveling salesman for the Liggett & Myers Tobacco Company, was one of them. It was love at first sight, and six months later they were married. My impulsive mother simply walked out of the flourishing Cat and Fiddle, gave it to her employees, and went off with my father, a handsome, soft-spoken, kindly man.

A year later, in 1925, my father bought a poolroom called Jack's Place in Wapato, 12 miles down the valley from Yakima. He did not serve women nor even allow them on the premises. Jack's Place was for men only. "The store," as we called it, had a long bar in the front on the left side with tall mirrors extending all the way to the ceiling and a lunch counter on the right side, opposite the bar. A partial partition at the end of the bar separated the front of the store from the back, where the poker and pool tables were. When the Crash came in 1929, the economy collapsed in Wapato, too. To stay in business, Pop cashed the farmworkers' meager paychecks, ran bank-nights when he gave away hams, turkeys and money as prizes to those who had a winning number on their ticket, and broadcast news and music over an outside loudspeaker. He was ahead of his time, running a small lottery to attract customers. In the difficult Depression years of the early 1930s, Pop also fed many hungry people who came to him for help.

From the time I was six, I often went behind the bar to get ice cream from the freezer to take home, and sometimes just to watch the goings-on. The bartenders didn't mind me standing near the big safe at the front end of the back bar while they served 14-ounce glasses of beer for 10 cents. One of their jobs was to keep trouble from happening, and if anyone started to get out of control, they threw them out. I especially remember the loaded Colt revolver that lay on the middle of the back bar. To my knowledge, it was never fired, but its presence was a deterrent that kept troublemakers from getting out of hand.

In 1934, Pop expanded into the slot-machine business and ran a string of penny, nickel, dime and quarter machines up and down the lower Yakima Valley. I was always thrilled when he let me count the pennies from the penny machines. When the slots were outlawed several years later, my resourceful father replaced them with pinball machines. While they weren't as profitable as their predecessors, they still made money.

Though Pop made a good living for us, Mama was very frugal. She paid only $20 a month rent for the little white house we lived in. Mama never had a washing machine; she did the laundry by hand and hung it outside to dry on the clothesline. We didn't have a radio; Mama thought Coco and I had better things to do. The arrival of the Sunday paper, the *Seattle Post Intelligencer,* which came 150 miles over the Cascade Mountains by train to our small town, was a big event. Each week I eagerly awaited the sports page and the funnies. Dick Tracy and Popeye were my favorites.

Our small hot-water tank was connected to the kitchen stove, a large and friendly wood-burning Monarch range with a big oven. Each evening when Coco and I were small, Mama carried large basins of hot water from that stove to the bathtub, where she would scrub us clean. The water was used twice.

One of my jobs from the age of seven on was to split wood for the stove, stack it in the garage, and keep the big woodbox in front of the hot-water tank filled. In winter, when I came in cold and shivering from playing outside in the snow, I loved to sit on the oven door of that mammoth stove and warm myself while the tea kettle purred back near the chimney. I can still recall how cozy it felt. My bed was on the front porch of our small house. There was no heat out there and the walls from the midpoint up to the ceiling were essentially open, being composed of only fine mesh wire screen. On cold winter nights I'd jump into bed and pump my legs up and down as fast as I could to warm the sheets, and then snuggle in and go to sleep.

In the front room, across from our small piano, there was a large, upright, rotund coke-burning stove that we filled from the top. Mama kept some of her first husband's medical books in a glass-fronted case in that room. From the time I was in fifth grade, I liked to take one of those big books from the case and settle down in the oversized leather rocking chair by the coke stove to read about strange diseases like tuberculosis and typhoid fever. I often felt as if I were looking at things I wasn't supposed to see. But I was fascinated by those books and kept being drawn to them. As I read I often wondered, "What would it be like to be a doctor and take care of sick people?"

Pop often took me hunting and fishing, and in the fall, he would sometimes even come to school in his hunting clothes and ask my teacher to let me out early, which she always did.

In the fall of 1934, when I was nearly eight, I vividly remember shooting my first pheasant, a big rooster with long, multicolored tail feathers. Somehow I hit this beautiful bird in the head with a single pellet from the 410-gauge shotgun Pop had given me, because it didn't kick too much. When I ran to my pheasant, then lifeless on the ground, I was both elated and sad at having killed this creature. Though that was 61 years ago, I can still feel the thrill of being with my dad on this and similar occasions that were special for a son to be with his father.

Each summer we had a two-month family vacation on Camano Island in Puget Sound. Pop and I loved to fish, and we caught great numbers of salmon in the waters around the island. But on Sunday morning we all spruced up, and Pop drove Mama, Coco and me to Mass some 30 miles away in Mt. Vernon. After Mass, Pop and I went back to fishing in our rented 16-foot kicker boat.

Pop's way of fishing was called "motor mooching." He used our boat's outboard motor to move the baited herring on our spinning gear, to make it look as if it were swimming. Pop ran the motor while I sat in the front of the boat and waited for a salmon to hit on my line. We took great pride in our large daily catch and felt especially good when we were the top boat on the beach, which we often were. Mama took equally great pleasure in giving most of our salmon away almost as soon as I had cleaned them. No doubt I developed some of my surgical skill from cleaning all those fish.

In those days I didn't like the taste of salmon. How I've changed! Now it's a delicacy that I relish for its flavor and because of its protective action in keeping my arteries healthy. I'm nostalgic for those days off Camano Island when I thrilled to the tug of a large salmon on my line, pole bent sharply and reel singing as a king salmon sounded deep or a hook-nose silver exploded into the air in a frantic leap.

Nearly every evening after dinner during our summer vacation, Coco and I walked to a lush, green meadow that was a mile down the shore from the little gray house that our folks rented for $100 a year. Deer were often in that meadow, munching away in the knee-high grass. On hearing us approach, they would raise their heads, look at us for a moment, and then continue eating as if we weren't there. After watching those gentle creatures for a few minutes, we headed home as the twilight moved toward darkness.

Mama made the rules for Coco and me. She was a deeply spiritual person who had been born into the Catholic faith and lived her religion, not as a badge on her blouse, but as a vital part of her being. God was a real and dynamic force to her, and He had that type of presence in our home as well. Pop had no formal religion when he married Mama, but he was a man of faith. He became a Catholic when I was ten, probably because of Mama's unending prayers. There was great joy in our family over that event.

In my childhood the Ten Commandments were regarded as stringent rules to follow in order to get to heaven. They told us what to do and what not to do. I understood that the punishment for failing to comply with these orders was hell, and I accepted this without question because of Mama. But I now appreciate the commandments as much more. I see them as the basic rules for proper human conduct, rules that if followed will enable us not only to enjoy the infinite rewards of heaven for all eternity, but also to experience great happiness here on earth.

Despite the austere spiritual force that ruled our home, Coco and I were happy. We had fun together, and our parents, while firm, were never mean. Only Mama applied discipline, and that was rare. She led us by her example, and she was led by Christ. Mama was a strong and happy woman; she understood and gratefully accepted her mission in life, which was to take care of her family.

Mama was a woman of action. If something needed to be done, she did it. She never bothered to consider the possible consequences of failure; she considered only the benefits of success. Mama had gone only as far as the third grade, but she was exceedingly intelligent and knew how to work. Pop's formal education had been of about the same length, and he was just as smart but in a different way. Where Mama was decisive, Pop was cautious. They made a great pair and complemented one another.

We lived on the edge of our small town, and I played for hours on end in the adjoining pasture and farmland. Once when I was about nine, I hid in the shelter of the tall cornfield behind our house and tried to smoke cigarettes. After sputtering and coughing over a few, I gave up and decided that smoking was not for me. My parents and Coco never knew about this experiment. On a healthier note, I recall how good the big, red Delicious apples tasted that I surreptitiously took each fall from an orchard about half a mile beyond the cornfield. Even now I smile when I eat an apple and remember crawling over the fence around that orchard to take the "forbidden fruit," then running like mad to get far away where I could catch my breath and enjoy my apple. I said nothing about this to anyone either.

I was approaching 13 years and about to enter the eighth grade when Hitler invaded Poland on September 1, 1939, and I had just turned 15 and was in the tenth grade when Japan attacked Pearl Harbor on December 7, 1941. The next summer

Mama decided that we would move to Spokane, 300 miles away, even though the United States was by then deeply embroiled in the throes of World War II. She arrived at her decision so that Coco and I could get a better education in the Catholic schools that were there. When she informed Pop of her plan, he grumbled at first, as he was prone to do, but he admired Mama for having the courage to make such a bold move. Gas was rationed and moving was a big deal. But with Mama at the helm, the deed was quickly done. Within days she had bought a new, three-bedroom house for $4,500 and moved us in. Coco began her freshman year at Holy Names College and, at 15, I began my junior year at Gonzaga High School, a Jesuit institution affiliated with Gonzaga University.

Father Mullins, the principal, and his staff ran a tight ship, and going to that high school would soon become a rude awakening for me. I'd never done any significant studying in the public school that Coco and I attended in Wapato, where my grades had been mainly C's and a few B's. But if I were to survive scholastically at Gonzaga, I quickly realized that I had to do what I had never done before—really apply myself. Further adding to my shock was the fact that discipline there was strict, forceful and timely. A few days after classes began, one of Father Mullins's Jesuit lieutenants called us together and said, "If any of you guys get out of line, we'll beat the hell out of you." I was shaken by this unequivocal statement of policy, but heedful of its meaning, I learned to study and managed to do well.

More important to me than my studies was the fact that in my junior year I was the number-two pitcher on the baseball team. I had good control, a sneaky fastball, a fair curveball, and a forkball that had some action. I wanted to become a Major League player—a pitcher like Dizzy Dean, or a hitter like Babe Ruth or even Joe DiMaggio. My favorite team was the St. Louis Cardinals. I looked forward to my senior year, when I could further indulge my fantasies about having a professional big-league career—fantasies that would soon come to an abrupt end. At the end of the baseball season in mid-May of 1943, Mama informed me that I was going to Gonzaga University starting in July.

I could skip my senior year of high school because I had enough credits to graduate at the end of my junior year. This was possible because when we lived in Wapato, our astute mother had taken Coco and me twice a week in the late afternoon for three years to a convent school ten miles away in Moxee, a small hop-growing community, where we studied French and Latin, subjects not taught in our public school. Mama thought that these languages were important for us to learn. There was no discussion; Coco and I did as we were told. But as a kid in knickerbockers, I hated those convent classes and would jump up and down on my books when no one was looking. Undoubtedly, Sister Eloise, our teacher, earned points for heaven by putting up with me. I could not have imagined then that those flattened books would become my ticket to the university and a head start toward medical school. Mama seemed to have had a premonition. Who's to know? But one thing is sure: without those language credits, I could not have gone to college that summer and as a result, may well have never become a doctor. At the time I had little enthusiasm for Mama's plan, since as a senior I would have been the starting pitcher for the baseball team. But this plan was not up for discussion either; I was going to college. After a couple of weeks I stopped complaining to myself and began to feel a sense of excitement about what lay ahead. Perhaps reading those old medical volumes had given me a deep, though still unformulated, desire to become a doctor. I registered as a premedical student. But at age 16 I was apprehensive, because I had no idea what going to the university would be like.

At that time the whole world was locked in the mortal combat of World War II. In Spokane, the U.S. Navy V-12 premedic program had taken over Gonzaga University. The navy's V-12 men were selected by competitive examination and sent to college as uniformed premedical students quartered on campus. They were put on an accelerated program, a new semester every four months. Those who did poorly returned to the fleet; those who did well continued through premedics and applied to medical schools for admission. If they were accepted, they went on to medical school at full government expense; if they weren't, they returned to the fleet. Those who graduated returned to the navy as medical officers. The V-12 program assured an adequate supply of high-quality physicians for the navy by providing medical schools with a pool of excellent applicants from which to make their selections. Without this and other comparable service programs, there would have been few medical students (and a postwar shortage of doctors), since all able-bodied men at age 18 were called up for military service. In order for me to receive a deferment from my draft board to continue my education, I had to be in medical school before I turned 18. But realistically there seemed little chance that I could meet the daunting schedule required to do this.

The V-12 men were the smartest, hardest-working students I have ever known, with a fierce work ethic motivated by the educational opportunity of their lives. They adopted me as a sort of mascot, since I was years younger than any of them and the only civilian in several of their classes. After a few weeks I got over the shock of being in college and evolved an intense study program, in which I seldom got to bed before 2:00 A.M. and was up again by 6:00.

I went to 6:30 Mass each morning at St. Aloysius, the college church. Going to daily Mass was a wonderful way of bonding with God and gaining inspiration for the day. During the first few months of premedics, I was torn between entering the Jesuit order and becoming a priest, or going on toward a career in medicine. I chose medicine because of an underlying conviction that I could do God's work best as a doctor. Thus, from the very beginning, my orientation toward medicine was deeply spiritual.

I took only the requirements for medical school, which at that time had been reduced to 60 semester hours of mainly science courses. Because of my draft deadline, I had to take all of my coursework in only three semesters. I have never worked harder than I did during that 12-month period. I got mainly A's and a few B's, and I also did well on the medical school aptitude examination. As a result, even though my chance of going to medical school had seemed remote when I started college, five first-rate schools accepted me: McGill University, the University of Southern California, Creighton University, Marquette University and St. Louis University. I selected St. Louis and left Spokane in mid-June of 1944 to become an inquisitive freshman medical student at the age of 17—two weeks after I should have graduated from high school and five months before I would be 18. Medical school would subsequently prove much easier for me than premed with the V-12 had been.

I remember the afternoon I boarded the *Empire Builder,* the crack Great Northern train to Chicago, and left Spokane to become a doctor. Me! The past year had gone so fast that it seemed a blur, hardly real. I transferred in Chicago to the Alton railroad and arrived in St. Louis in the late afternoon of a smotheringly hot and humid summer day. It seemed as if I had stepped into a sweltering sauna when I got off that air-conditioned train. Although I came to love St. Louis and my medical school, I never got used to the Mississippi River-bottom summers.

My days in medical school were intense, but less so than my premed year had been. My deductive and introspective talents were well-suited to learning how the human body functions. I learned best by spending some time every night studying each subject, rather than by concentrating for many hours on one subject. Instead of cramming for exams, I got more sleep than usual the night before. The study habits I developed in medical school, while unusual for most med students, would play a vital role later on in helping me run a busy surgical practice while developing and directing a major research institute at the same time.

During the late 1930s and throughout the 1940s, studies on animals were paving the way for the development of an exciting new specialty for humans—cardiovascular surgery. Progress in this rapidly developing field would soon produce dramatic advances that would electrify the medical world. These brilliant accomplishments reflected the daring skill of the surgical pioneers of those challenging days and the unswerving faith of the patients and their families. The "miracle" operations that they astutely devised and boldly performed corrected abnormalities of the big vessels near the heart, increased the oxygen content in the blood of some types of "blue babies," and enlarged the restricted opening of narrowed valves by dilating them with a finger or instrument placed within the heart. Dr. Robert E. Gross, developer of two of these "miracle" operations and chief of surgery at Boston Children's Hospital, was one of the great pioneers of that remarkable period. Little did I dream that several years later I would train under this surgical giant.

There was an enormous sense of excitement in the medical world of the late 1940s, in anticipation of the era of open-heart surgery that was about to begin. This development had been considered in prior years to be beyond the surgeon's realm. Now it was at hand. But even the visionaries of the 1940s couldn't fully perceive the total significance of this oncoming epic advance—that it would ultimately allow the human heart to be stopped, opened, repaired and restarted, or, if necessary, even to be replaced. But first the heart-lung machine had to be developed and progressively refined. Concomitant with this great step, similar advances would be required in surgical techniques, anesthetic management and pharmacologic agents. These developments would begin to reach patients in the early 1950s, accelerate in the 1960s and 1970s, and continue into the 1980s and 1990s, so that today there is almost nothing about the heart that cannot be repaired or replaced.

By my senior year in medical school I was determined to become a surgeon and graduated near the top of my class in June 1948, at age 21. I was accepted for internship at the highly reputed King County Hospital in Seattle, where I continued to apply my proven formula of hard work, and was accepted into the University of Washington General Surgery residency at King County under Dr. Henry N. Harkins, a remarkable man and the first professor of surgery at the newly created University of Washington School of Medicine. He recognized my introspective talents and guided me into surgical research, which was a happy and important part of my professional life throughout my clinical career, and continues to be so now on a full-time basis in my "retirement."

My surgical residency was interrupted in 1952 when I was called into the Army Medical Corps as a lieutenant during the Korean War. I was initially scheduled to join the surgical research team in Korea, but was reassigned to the Army Medical Services Graduate School at the Walter Reed Army Medical Center in Washington, D.C., where I spent two years. There I had the good fortune to plan and conduct an important experimental vascular surgery research program. My experiments involved the study of blood vessel grafts that I placed into the big artery, called the aorta, in the chest of young pigs. To get the pigs for my experiments, I went out into the Maryland countryside and caught them.

A high-spirited enlisted man and I would put on overalls, get an army truck, and head out into the farm country. When we found a farm with little pigs, we stopped and struck a deal with the farmer. Then we jumped into the pen and had great fun catching the most energetic and loudly squealing ones, weighing from 20 to 35 pounds, as they ran madly about with my assistant and me in hot pursuit. After paying the going rate to the farmer for those we had captured, we moved on to the next farm. When we had caught our quota, we returned to stately Walter Reed with our load of from 30 to 50 noisy, hungry pigs. Getting those little beasts out of the truck and safely into their pens was also a challenge, but once they had enjoyed their first army chow, our piglets bedded down contentedly and adjusted to their new surroundings.

The Army Medical Service Graduate School had never experienced anything like those little pigs before, nor, I suspect, has it since. I liked my pigs and took good care of them. I have always felt that if one does research on animals, they must be taken care of in the kindest manner possible.

I implanted 15 series of different kinds of arterial grafts in over 200 of my little pigs. A few days later when they had recovered from their surgeries, I sent them to a farm in Maryland about 20 miles outside of Washington, D.C., where they grew up like regular pigs. Six to eight months later, when they weighed 200 pounds or more, I sent six of them at a time for slaughter, each Tuesday and Thursday morning for five months, to a huge packing plant in Baltimore, where they would be the first of 2,000 pigs to be processed that day.

I had to be at the plant by 6:00 A.M. and left Washington at 4:30 so as not to be late. Once that processing line got started it could not be stopped to wait for me. But the men on the line had great interest in those "army pigs" and helped me remove the blood vessel grafts I had implanted in their aortas. After recovering the grafts, I returned to Walter Reed and spent most of the next 24 hours studying them. I summed up the voluminous observations made from these investigations and reported them in a major paper entitled "The Healing and Fate of Arterial Grafts," which was published in a leading surgical journal in 1955. That army project initiated my subsequent lifelong research in developing improved synthetic replacements for diseased arteries.

While in the army, I came to a decision that would shape the rest of my life. I decided to specialize in both pediatric (children's) and cardiovascular surgery, and wondered if I could train in children's surgery, both general and cardiac, under the world-renowned Dr. Gross in Boston after I had finished my adult general and vascular surgery training under the noted Dr. Harkins in Seattle. Because the answer to this question was so critical to my future, I went to Boston in September of 1954 and asked Dr. Gross if he would accept me into his senior residents program in July of 1956. My elation knew no bounds when he said, "Yes," and I returned to Walter Reed with great enthusiasm for the challenges that lay ahead. After completing my two-year tour of army duty in December of 1954, I was discharged as a captain and returned to Seattle to complete my training under Dr. Harkins, being scheduled to finish in June of 1956.

But soon after I was back in Seattle something happened to me—something wonderful! I met the girl who means everything to me—the girl who would become my wife. When I think about how close I came to never meeting her, a chill runs through me. Shortly after starting my first rotation, a three-month assignment at the Seattle Children's Hospital, I had a date with an attractive student from Seattle University. After seeing the movie *Brigadoon,* we walked by a photography studio where I just happened to look at the display window and see the portrait of a most beautiful young woman. There was something so special about the girl in this photograph that I couldn't restrain myself from exclaiming about her to my date. To my great surprise and enormous pleasure, my date said that she knew her. Somehow I managed to say, "What's her name?"

"Mary Ann Marti," she said. My date also told me that Mary Ann was a nursing student and the homecoming queen at Seattle University. I was deeply grateful for this information, but I didn't quite know how to thank my date under the circumstances!

The next two nights were crazy. The first night I paced the floor of my room at Children's Hospital until it was too late to call this girl of my dreams. My resolve gained strength throughout the next day as, preoccupied, I did my work, and by nightfall I was ready. I made *the* call to Seattle University Information and was told, "Miss Marti can be reached at the nursing school residence."

Nothing was going to stop me now.

With my heart pounding wildly when I heard her beautiful voice on the other end of the line, I made a most direct statement. The words just came out; I had not rehearsed them: "Miss Marti, if you are not married, engaged or otherwise spoken for, I would greatly appreciate meeting you."

I suspect she thought I was completely off my rocker, but being adventuresome she said that she would meet me, though I'd have to call back in a couple of days for the time. In the meantime my resourceful wife-to-be checked with the University of Washington to see if they really had a surgical resident by the name of Lester Sauvage. When she found that they did, she then wisely sought her mother's advice. The net result was that when I called back two days later, she suggested that I come to her parents' home to meet her. I can still feel the thrill of that moment when I first saw my sweetheart. Not only was she beautiful, but she had goodness written all over her.

After that we began to date, and two weeks later I told her we would be going to Boston in June of 1956. She was so startled by this enigmatic announcement that she nearly stopped seeing me. But she got over her surprise, and we continued dating. I had fallen in love with my Mary Ann from the instant I had first seen her picture. I can't explain what happened to me, but it's true. I knew from that moment that she was the one and only girl for me. My problem was to convince her that I was the one and only boy for her. To my great joy, I could tell as the months passed that she was falling in love with me, too.

She said yes when I proposed just before Christmas in 1955, and June 9, 1956 remains the greatest day of my life, for on that date I married my sweetheart, a loving and radiant young nurse destined to specialize in pediatrics, in a manner of speaking, with our eight children with whom we would subsequently be blessed. Mary Ann is the most wonderful wife, mother and now grandmother to 14 grandchildren that there could possibly be. She is my best friend, and I love her with all my heart and soul. Over the nearly 40 years of our marriage, our love has grown ever deeper. Little things become more precious day by day, like saying "I love you, Sweetheart" when I leave home in the morning and when I return in the evening, regardless of the hour.

In late June of 1956, after our honeymoon in Victoria on Vancouver Island, Mary Ann and I left for Boston (as I had told her we would!), where I was to begin my residency on July 1st at the Children's Hospital under Dr. Gross, professor of surgery at the Harvard Medical School.

But before leaving for Boston, one of Seattle's leading surgeons, who was also chief of heart surgery at the Children's Hospital in Seattle, offered me the opportunity to join his practice on my return with the clear understanding that I would be in charge of *developing and directing* the open-heart surgery program at Children's. This was the opportunity I had dreamt about, and I enthusiastically accepted his offer. The emerging field of open-heart surgery was then in the early days of its exciting development in Boston, and my training there would prepare me for the responsibilities that would be mine when we returned home.

Dr. Gross was exceedingly kind to me, and in my second year he offered me the great opportunity to stay with him at Boston Children's Hospital. Also, during that same year, Dr. C. Rollins Hanlon, professor of surgery at my medical school, invited me to join him at St. Louis University. But I had given my word. There was no question—we would return home and develop the open-heart program for Children's Hospital in Seattle.

Our Boston days were full of happiness, excitement, learn-ing, adventure and challenge. The future seemed boundless. After completing my training there in December 1958, Mary Ann and I headed west to Seattle to begin our new life, accompanied by our first child, a baby boy, Lester Jr., now a board-certified internist and geriatrician.

When we arrived home, I was full of anticipation and energy to begin development of the program at Children's Hospital. But I soon found, to my complete dismay, that every-thing had changed. Though my name was on the door and on the stationery of the prestigious surgeon's office and the announcements of my joining his practice had been sent out, things were not right. I had accepted the position on good faith, with the explicit understanding that I would inaugurate and run the open-heart surgery service at Children's on my return to Seattle. Despite this agreement, the surgeon and his staff had proceeded to launch the program a few weeks before I was to arrive without so much as notifying me. In that short time they had performed surgery on seven children, and all had died. When I inquired about my previously agreed-upon status as *developer and director* of the program, the surgeon informed me that he had changed his mind. I was instead to work my way up as one of his assistants. I was stunned.

I went home and told Mary Ann what had happened and what the surgeon had said. Though we agonized over this for the next two days, there was no question—I would leave his firm. The following afternoon, though beset with much trepidation, I went back to the surgeon's office and told him, "Because you have changed the conditions that we agreed on without my consent, I must resign from your office." He became furious, while my fright escalated still more. I quickly turned and walked out, thankful that this awful moment was over.

The full impact of what had transpired became ever more obvious to me during the next few days. I had burned my bridges behind me when we came West. I had declined Dr. Gross's invitation to stay at Boston Children's Hospital and had declined Dr. Hanlon's invitation to join him in St. Louis. Now I desperately hoped that one or both of those opportunities might still be available to me. I tactfully inquired. Neither was. And now there was no place for me in Seattle, either. A sense of hopelessness settled over me as my once-lofty goals, noble purposes and self-confidence quickly disappeared. I soon felt that I had no worth, became deeply depressed, and for the first time in my life experienced total frustration. By then I was afraid even to appear at hospital conferences. I stayed home because I was empty and frightened. I couldn't sleep, yet I was exhausted. The spark was gone. I was lost. I didn't know what to do or where to go. For two terrible months I knew the depths of despair. It was an awful experience that I hope I'll never have to endure again.

Mary Ann was very worried about me, but she never let on. She told me over and over that everything would be alright. She was right. With her help I slowly began to come out of my shell, and after several weeks, life began to look a little better. But had it not been for Dr. Alexander Bill, a noted pediatric surgeon in Seattle who took me into his practice, I don't know what might have happened to me. His support helped me at the very time in my life when I needed help the most. Over the course of the next few weeks, my confidence slowly returned as my depression disappeared. By spring I was back to normal. It was wonderful to have a buoyant spirit once again, and through the grace of God, I have never been depressed since.

Even with Dr. Bill's help, my surgical career in Seattle

started slowly. It was two-pronged from the beginning—
patient care and research. That spring, I began my surgical
practice at Providence and Children's Hospitals, and within a
few months established a small surgical research laboratory
adjacent to Providence in an empty, old, but sturdy house that
the hospital owned. Our first experiments were directed
toward two goals: developing a method for repairing leaky
heart valves with tissue from the sac around the heart, the peri-
cardium, and learning how best to design artificial arteries.
This research lab was initially part of the hospital, but over the
years it has evolved into a much larger independent research
organization now known as The Hope Heart Institute. Bob
Hope helped the Institute by allowing us to use his name in our
title. In addition, from the mid-1970s to the early-1980s, he
was personally involved in many supportive ways, including
financial. We shall always be indebted to him. With his con-
currence we have continued to use "Hope" in the Institute's
name, but now in the context of the theological virtues of
Faith, Hope and Charity.

I did general pediatric surgery at Children's and cardiovascular surgery at Providence in my early practice years, being
excluded from the heart service at Children's by staff politics.
Though my practice grew slowly for the first several years, my
research program not only grew rapidly in those early years, it
has continued to progress beyond my most optimistic expecta-
tions. My staff and I have developed new surgical concepts,
operations, surgical devices, blood tests and medications.
These advances include an operation to repair leaky heart
valves; the world's first experimental use of vein grafts to
increase blood flow to the arteries of the heart; the trellis concept of assisted cellular migration that formed the basis for the
design of the Sauvage line of synthetic blood-vessel grafts,

which are still manufactured and distributed world-wide by C. R. Bard, Inc.; an operation to share the abundant blood supply of an arm with that of the impoverished lower limbs of fragile, elderly patients, enabling them to walk, sleep and avoid amputations; a test to measure the tendency of an individual's blood platelets to form life- and limb-endangering clots; drugs to prevent such clotting from occurring; and the world's first use of both internal mammary arteries (small vessels located in the front of the chest, one to each side of the breast bone) to restore circulation to the *entire* heart. It is a technique that rarely requires reoperation because these grafts seldom close off, in contrast to the frequent closure after several years of vein grafts taken from the legs. I performed my first human coronary bypass graft in May 1968, followed by two more in the next few weeks. Each was successful, and the second patient continues in good health now 28 years later.

In 1970, I was surprised and very pleased when I was asked by the hospital board to become the chief of cardiac surgery at Children's. I accepted this added responsibility, even though by then I had become very busy taking care of adult heart patients at Providence and running the expanding research programs of the Institute.

Because of my increasing work load I added my first partner in 1971 and eventually six more, all of whom possessed great talent and flourished. None left to practice elsewhere, a fact of which I'm very proud. Despite the addition of these remarkable men, the demands on my time did not lessen because all our practices continued to grow.

I performed the best operation I could for each patient, regardless of the time or effort it took. Early on I appreciated that there was far more to surgery than the details of incisions, grafts and stitches. There was the human dimension. The night before a patient's operation, generally toward ten o'clock, I called the husband or wife to say that I was confident God would hear our prayers and guide our work for his or her loved one.

Despite my words of reassurance, the day of surgery was nonetheless a time of intense worry for the family and friends that waited. During the surgery, I sent periodic messages to ease their fears. After the surgery, I went to the waiting room as soon as I could and told them how the patient was doing, what we had done, and the progress they could expect in the next few days. I then took them into the intensive care unit to see their loved one. In the ensuing days I called or saw the family and friends as often as I could. In the event that a patient was doing poorly, I intensified their care and increased the frequency of talking with the family. I often thought, "How would I be if my Mary Ann were the patient?" That thought alone helped me realize that I was nearly always taking care of more than one person.

I spent long hours at the hospital and developed the reputation of prowling the halls in the early morning hours. I often found my patients awake and frequently noted some aspect of their care that needed adjustment. And they appreciated hearing my words of reassurance followed by a pleasant "good night and happy dreams." After finishing my late rounds, I would usually spend an hour or two in the research institute reading and answering correspondence, planning experiments, reviewing data, preparing presentations and working on papers before I went home. I followed this schedule because I had no other time, and as a result, I seldom got home before 2:00 A.M.

While my practice and research demands were mounting, Mary Ann and I were blessed with seven additional children after Lester Jr. But my time for family and for patients and research was coming into increasing conflict, and resolving that dilemma became top priority for Mary Ann and me. A solution was possible because we viewed all we did as a mutual effort, whether family, patient care or research. In my mind, Mary Ann was part of all I did, and in her mind, I was part of all she did. I told her about our patients and research, and she told me about our children. The children knew we deeply loved each other and that we both loved each of them. They knew that their mother supported all I did and that I supported all she did. Mother made the rules in our home and I backed them up. Though I was away much of the time, we were nonetheless together as a family. We agreed that my primary job was to take care of our patients and our research work, and hers was to take care of our children and our home. The fact that we lived only five minutes away from the hospital and research institute (and still do—in the same house) helped by making it possible for me to get home on some evenings during the week for brief periods.

Though I wish I could have had more time with Mary Ann and our children, I did what I could. I looked forward to being with them in the early morning when they were getting up. When I could get home in the evening, we had some great games of "horse" in our outdoor basketball court. I had more time with the family on Sundays and holidays, unless I was on call or in surgery. Despite my absences, our family was and continues to be successful because of the great goodness of Mary Ann, who regarded the raising of our children as a sacred vocation. She taught and radiated love to them. Thanks to her caring and skill, they are all fine young men and women today.

Despite her countless activities with the children, Mary Ann somehow managed to take the best care of me as well.

There was always a delicious dinner waiting for me in the early morning hours of those practice years when I got home. Her talents didn't stop there. She has looked after our business affairs so efficiently that I have seldom had to even write a check. In fact, I have given attention only to the broad aspects of our financial matters. In addition, Mary Ann was a volunteer nurse at the St. Joseph's grade school during most of the years our children were there. Subsequently, she was involved in board responsibilities in their high school (Seattle Prep) and later their university (Seattle U), where she is still involved. Because of her love of music, she also served for many years on the board of the Seattle Youth Symphony Orchestra. Further, for the past 35 years she has been an active member of the Association for Catholic Childhood here in Seattle. And during my surgical career, Mary Ann was always at my side to comfort me on those infrequent but exceedingly sad occasions when I lost a patient. Her words and presence encouraged me to continue our research so that the failure of that day would not have been in vain and could lead instead to the successes of tomorrow. Quite simply, Mary Ann is an amazing woman.

Our annual August vacations and several overseas trips that we took together were special family occasions. While our foreign adventures didn't make up for my being at the hospital and institute so much of the time when we were home, they helped, for on those excursions I was totally involved with the family without any outside interruptions. In all, we made nine such trips to various distant parts of the world, with each lasting from two to three weeks. In aggregate, those trips extended across four continents. Five were built around overseas speaking engagements of mine. We took all eight of our children with us on the first four trips, seven on the fifth, and lesser numbers on the rest (we took all who could come). On several of those trips, we also took two or three other family members with us (my dad and Mary Ann's mother, father or her sister, Rosie, a nun). Our guide and driver, who were always at the airport to meet us when we arrived abroad, never had any trouble identifying our distinctive group when we came off the plane. For example, on our first trip in 1975, the ages of our extended family ranged from 4 to 84 years. Once we were under way, our guide and driver became part of the family for the rest of that journey. We traveled together in a personal bus across the countryside, from city to city, as we visited one historic site after another.

We traveled to Rome, Assisi (home of St. Francis), the French Riviera, Greece, the Greek Islands and 16 other countries, from Sweden to New Zealand to Thailand. Once we spent three weeks in Israel and traced Christ's path. On that trip our youngest daughter made her first Holy Communion at Midnight Mass on Christmas Eve in the Church of the Nativity in Bethlehem, while armed Israeli troops stood guard in the courtyard and at the doors inside. The last trip when all the children could come with us was to Hawaii, and then on to Japan. Those trips were great family experiences and the best form of education for all of us. While they were expensive, those expeditions were a bargain in terms of the priceless memories that remain with each of us today, and we often talk about them.

All eight of our children now live in Seattle and seven are married. We get together at our home every month or two for combined birthday celebrations, which are happy times of fun and sharing with lots of small children running around. We also still look forward to our annual August vacation at our summer retreat on the straits of Juan de Fuca, 70 miles northwest of

Seattle. Those are precious days when we can all be together. We play games, walk, run, swim, ride bicycles, tell stories, go fishing, catch crabs, eat together, pray together and just plain enjoy one another.

Coincident with the evolving events in my family life, the demands on my professional time by the mid-1970s had become so intense that I either had to make some drastic changes or run the risk of having an accident in the operating room from being overextended. I was determined that this would not occur. I clearly remember the early morning when I took my first major step to resolve this problem. I called Dr. Stanley Stamm, Chief of Medical Cardiology at Children's Hospital, and told him that I was stepping down as Chief of Cardiac Surgery at Children's in favor of my first partner, Dr. Peter Mansfield. This helped for a time, but a few years later I found that it was no longer enough. I had by then run out of time again and realized that I couldn't continue going to both hospitals. This fact forced me to make the even more difficult decision of which one I would stop going to. Though I dearly loved my work with children, I couldn't drop my adult work and its associated research. I had no choice. Reluctantly, I stopped going to Children's entirely in 1980 and turned my practice there over to two of my other partners.

From that time on I restricted my practice to adult cardio-vascular surgery and research, confining my time to the Providence Medical Center and The Hope Heart Institute, which is located adjacent to the hospital. Despite this consol-idation, the increasing scope of my practice and the expand-ing research programs of the Institute, my normal workday, usually seven days a week, still averaged 20 hours. Usually I got home between 2:00 and 3:00 A.M. and left again by 6:30 A.M. By 1990 unmistakable signs that I needed more rest had begun to appear. I noticed that I was less efficient late at night than I had been the year before, and it was harder to get up after three hours of sleep than it had been six months previously. These warning signals told me that I couldn't continue my intense schedule for more than a year or two and still give my patients the quality care they deserved. Rather than slow down, my hope was to work full tilt right up to the end, do as perfect an operation for my last patient as I had ever done for anyone, and then retire to full-time research. I wanted to be able to remember my last year in practice with joy.

Selecting the time to stop doing something you love to do is difficult. But I was driven by the fear that I might wait too long and injure someone. Even so, I found it easy to ignore the fact that time was passing and my skills could be receding. But Mary Ann and I realized we had to face this important issue and began to seriously consider it from the time I reached 60. We spent long hours discussing the right time for me to stop doing clinical surgery and in 1989 decided that my last case would be on November 30, 1991, two weeks after I turned 65. (I will tell you how suddenly stopping what I had done for 33 years affected me in my comments after the last patient's story—Chapter 12.)

The reality of the years was also becoming apparent to us in the aging of our parents. While Mary Ann and I were advancing into the mid-part of our earthly journeys, both of my parents and Mary Ann's mother were moving into the terminal part of theirs. My mother died of leukemia at age 78. Her last days were not easy. Chemotherapy made her mouth raw and caused all her beautiful, long, gray-tinged dark hair to fall out. She ordered a matching wig and wore it so her stark appearance would not be so hard on my father. Mama never complained and was lucid to the end. She didn't fear death; her faith sustained her.

After Mama died, my father lived his last 13 years with us. He died at 94, not of disease but of advanced old age, in his own bed, at our home. When he died he was but a shell of his former self, having lost much weight in his last few weeks. In those terminal days he still ate ice cream, but it did him little good. It was as if his cells had turned off. Their time had come to die.

We took turns being with him. When he died at 2:00 A.M., his grandson John, age 25, was at his side holding his hand. Johnny came to our room and, sobbing, told us, "Grandpa's gone." The morticians came and put his withered form in their body bag, placed him on their small stretcher, and were out the front door in minutes. We heard their motor start and then they were gone, leaving behind only the deafening silence of death. We cried and felt alone, despite knowing that the time for his transition to eternity had come.

During the years Pop lived with us, he contributed much to his grandchildren. They still speak of him with deep affection in their adult years, and remember the beautiful hook-nose silver salmon he caught every fall until he was 90. Pop left his mark on all of us.

My wife's mother, whom we called Ranny, was an avid gardener and talented pianist, a loving wife, mother and grandmother, and courageous to the end. She died of cancer of the pancreas at age 76. She had undergone surgery but to no avail; the tumor had spread to her liver. Chemotherapy was ineffective and only made her worse. She knew that death was near. We took her to our home so she could go in peace. One morning she heard the doorbell ring and thought her doctor, whom she liked, was coming to see her. She said, "Don't let him in, I'm ready to go to God. It's time."

She died a few days later, on a sunny spring morning, with

her husband, children and grandchildren all around her. There was a gentle peace as this gracious lady moved to eternity. Her life was a job well done.

We grieved deeply when our parents died. Even now I have tears in my eyes as I think of them and write these words. As time moves on for Mary Ann and me, seemingly with increasing speed, we ask in wonderment, "Where have those precious days gone?"

Mary Ann's father, now 88, prefers to live alone in his own home, where he cares for Ranny's beautiful garden. Though he finds this harder now, he is still doing well, a tribute to his faith and courage. When the weather is pleasant and the daylight hours long, he frequently drives over to join us for Sunday dinner, and these are special times for us. In the winter Mary Ann drives to his home and brings him to ours. Papa's mind is sharp and his views on current events are well worth listening to.

It's hard to believe that my sister is now 71 and I am 69, for it seems like yesterday we were children at home in Wapato. Coco married Al Fetchko, a medical-school classmate of mine, who recently retired from his practice of obstetrics and gynecology. They have lived in Natrona Heights, a suburb of Pittsburgh, since 1948, and have raised a fine family. Like Mary Ann and me, Coco and Al are now in the grandchildren phase of their lives.

As my journey of life continues, my belief in God is what matters most to me. My happiness results from my faith in Jesus Christ as true God and true man, from my life with Mary Ann, from the love within our family, from the challenges of the extensive research programs I direct at The Hope Heart Institute, and from the good I can do for others. My spiritual growth through the years has enabled me to increasingly enjoy each moment of life and, at the same time, to approach eternity with an emerging anticipation of the infinite peace that awaits us all if we do God's work in this world with love in our hearts.

Finding the Spirit Within

Lester Sauvage, M.D.

In the course of doing open-heart surgery for 33 years, I became keenly aware that my patients and I needed to be concerned about more than merely extending the length of our physical lives. We had need to be concerned about experiencing increased happiness in those extended years if this added time was to be truly meaningful to us.

In my career I progressed to understand that optimal health is much more than the mere absence of disease. I came to appreciate that it is being all we can be, both physically and spiritually. Medical science now recognizes that the body and the spirit interact, and that a happy spirit can help heal the body and then assist in keeping it healthy.

And I advanced more. I came to perceive that I had a unique opportunity as an open-heart surgeon to assist my patients with achieving the objective of optimal health during the time I had the privilege of caring for them. Over many years of doing surgery I learned that in order to help my patients attain this goal, I had to not only provide superb care for their physical needs, but I had to give sensitive attention to their spiritual needs as well. In this context I'm not talking about specific religious dogma, but rather to the universal needs of our human spirit for love, concern, care, kindness and dignity. This comprehensive management plan fills the void that patients feel when their doctors are too busy to treat them as people with problems and instead treat them as impaired mechanical parts that need to be fixed. This disparaging practice occurs when we hear patients referred to as "that heart in 202," "that stroke in 404" or "that leg in 606." To assist my patients in focusing the spiritual dimensions of their lives as they pursued the goal of optimal health, I asked them to answer the following three questions for themselves:

What will I do with the added years that surgery will bring?
How will I find increased happiness in these "extra years"?
What is happiness to me?

Most of my patients found that pondering these questions helped them in this combined body-soul process of becoming all they could be. They found that it gave greater sharpness to the purpose of their lives, decreased their anxiety, and increased their determination to get well quickly and move on with their lives. I firmly believe that patients who go to surgery in this manner do better than those who go in a highly anxious and uncertain state. I strove to get my patients in the best physical and mental shape that I could before their surgeries and then did the technical aspects of their operations to the best of my ability. Much of my success and happiness as a heart surgeon was the result of developing this combined approach to patient care.

My Christian faith was strengthened as a result of these spiritual interactions with my patients. While I was opening their physical hearts, they were opening my spiritual heart. And as they did this to me, I became better able to help them open theirs. In the course of our interactions, my patients and I found that implementing a three-step spiritual action plan that reflected the generic teachings of all the great religions of humankind was the surest way for us to experience increased happiness in our own lives. These steps are:

1. Embrace each day to the fullest.
2. Talk to God and listen, too.
3. Serve God by serving humanity.

When I talked to my patients—whether they were Jewish, Buddhist, Hindu, Christian, Muslim, agnostic, atheist or other—about spiritual matters, I was careful to respect their private beliefs, and they respected mine. It was this mutual respect that enabled us to feel comfortable and enjoy our discussions.

I found the words of Christ and of Gandhi very helpful in initiating these spiritual discussions with my patients. I reminded them that Christ, the Son of God, said, "Whatsoever you do unto the least of these you do unto Me," and that many centuries later Gandhi said, "If you don't see God in the very next person you meet, it's a waste of time to look further." The message is clear: *God is omnipresent and is the Spirit*

within your soul and mine. God awaits within for us to find
and follow Him. This truth enables me to love you, myself
and every human being. God asks us to tend his flock, and He
rewards us with happiness when we do. To me happiness is
that peace of mind, serenity of soul, and exhilaration of spirit
that God gives us when we, out of love, serve those who need
us. And the simple truth is that we all need one another.
Indeed, our soul's need to achieve and sustain this vibrant
state of happy consciousness is as great as our body's need for
food and water.

In the main, our affluent contemporary society seeks meaning and fulfillment through material goods, but it is finding
this approach increasingly disappointing. Each of us has an
innate longing for "something else," something that "material
things" can't provide—"soul things." But our materialistic
culture makes us self-conscious and hesitant to express our
belief in God and a life hereafter. We tend to keep secret those
aspects of our lives that lie at the core of our being.

I have found when I speak to lay audiences about heart
problems that I can often bring them to their feet with excited
applause at the conclusion of my presentation, by combining
scientific facts with the spiritual insights that have contributed
to my own philosophy of life. In the course of such an address
I tell them that each of us answers only the following four
fundamental questions during our lives:

1. What shall I do to earn my daily bread?
2. Where will I do this?
3. Whom shall I ask to be or accept as my life's partner?
4. Why do I want to live at all?

I tell my audiences that everything I have done in my life
is, in some way or another, an attempt to answer one or the

other of these questions. Further, I tell them that it is only through the helping of others that any of us will find happiness in our lives. Also, after I explain that happy people tend to enjoy better physical health because of their positive mental attitude, my audiences show even greater interest in the spiritual dimensions of their lives. But in the question-and-answer session that follows, the great majority of these same people squelch their response to the spiritual and ask me only questions like, "How much salt may I have?" or "My cholesterol is 210, what should I do?" I don't mean to imply that these questions are unimportant, but there is more to life than salt and cholesterol.

Though my listeners appreciate knowing my generic spiritual views, most of them are reluctant to reveal theirs. In my early practice years, I, too, found it difficult to divulge mine, but after interacting with my patients over many years, I became less hesitant about doing so and more skilled in weaving spiritual matters into the fabric of our discussions.

I told my patients that I couldn't believe in God or eternity if it were not for my faith. When I look to the heavens on a clear, dark night and see the Milky Way and a myriad of other stars millions of light-years away, twinkling in the vastness of the universe, I know that God exists, though I don't know how or why. But this belief enables me to accept that God and eternity are real and reminds me of the story of the man standing on the beach, trying unsuccessfully to put the ocean into a small, leaky bucket. When he found that he couldn't do it, he refused to accept that the ocean existed. My mind's capacity in relation to God and eternity is like that of the man's small leaky bucket in relation to the vast ocean. But unlike that man, I believe in the reality of God and eternity, even though my mind lacks the capacity to contain these mysteries. My faith in these vital matters gives me hope that I have a future beyond the grave.

After having thoroughly discussed the diagnosis and treatment of their heart problems, I found that asking my patients, *"Why do you want to live longer?"* was a direct way to get our spiritual discussions going. To the best of my knowledge I never offended a single patient by asking them this question, though some were momentarily startled by it. Admittedly, though, many must have wondered at first what I was trying to get at. But my patients soon came to appreciate that this introspection helped them answer the question, *"What am I going to do with the added years that my operation will bring me?"* Furthermore, this thought-provoking question opened the door to many other questions, including, *"Why do I do what I do?"* and *"What is happiness to me?"* This discussion enabled us to acknowledge that money, power, fame and prestige, in and of themselves, are unable to bring this priceless treasure into our lives. Instead, our discussion led us to identify that happiness is a state of mind that comes to us only through love and sharing.

As we talked, my patients soon came to appreciate that we were discussing what they were going to be doing *after* their surgeries. They realized that I expected them to live, and this realization had a major impact on their frame of mind before surgery: "He expects me to survive—hurray!" Suddenly they gained confidence in their futures. Many other benefits accrued to my patients because I paid *some* attention to the broad spiritual dimensions of their lives, while I was giving *intense* attention to the details of their physical care. This encompassing approach enabled my patients to gain an increased sense of direction and purpose for their lives, to anticipate being active participants in the additional years I was helping them achieve, and to develop a greater willingness to think about their ultimate destiny. What I did for their spirit was not difficult and can be done by any physician. In fact, many doctors do everything I did, and some do more. All that a physician need do is commit to caring, take the extra step when necessary, and develop a proper sense of timing for discussion of spiritual subjects with his or her patients.

Nonetheless, there is no question that the process of assisting my patients in their spiritual explorations and reassessments when they were preparing to undergo heart surgery was challenging both to them and to me. The approach to each patient is different. In the next chapter you'll read how I proceeded with Joe, a wealthy businessman from Bernardsville, New Jersey, who presented some of the most difficult psychological and surgical problems that I ever encountered. You'll see that taking care of Joe's heart would have been impossible without first helping him take care of his spirit. He was a fragile, frightened, depressed human being who also happened to have terrible heart disease. Though he desperately needed coronary bypass surgery to bring new blood supply to his impoverished heart, it was clear that he first needed to regain a sense of high purpose in his life so that he could once more come to appreciate, at least in part, his infinite worth as an instrument of God's work in this world. Only then could he face the reality of his physical condition and accept the treatment that was necessary to improve it.

In the early years of my practice, it was hard for me to tell a patient, "I believe in God and in a life beyond this" because I felt self-conscious and exposed in making such a statement. Without question, spiritual affirmations are difficult for many physicians to make. In fact, without personal commitment and preparation, such dialogue with a patient may be impossible.

Fortunately, when I took care of Joe, I had progressed beyond that point.

Once I had convinced him to regard his glass of life as half full rather than half empty, we could begin to talk about his future and what he wanted it to be. As our discussions progressed, I could sense that Joe was gradually coming to accept that the time away from the distractions of his daily life that surgery would impose on him could be used instead for personal reflection and spiritual growth. As our long-distance friendship developed, I could perceive that Joe was beginning to gain some appreciation of each day as an opportunity to experience happiness by serving God in this world. He was coming to recognize that eternity was his destiny, and this life could be a joyous journey to get there.

In times of crisis our nature forces us to lean on someone or something. We are all fragile and dependent. Joe had to lean on me because we met at a threatening time in his life. To obtain the mental peace he needed in order to submit to the surgery he required, Joe had to believe that I could do no wrong. It was good that he didn't know how fragile I was, too.

We all have to struggle if we are to reduce our human fragilities. Since 1975 I have obtained great help in my efforts to do this by saying the prayer of St. Francis of Assisi. St. Francis was a humble man who understood life and his own weaknesses. From that dual understanding and with the grace of God, he was blessed with great inner power. His beautiful prayer, "Lord, Make Me an Instrument of Your Peace," says it all:

Prayer of St. Francis

Lord, make me an instrument
of your peace.

Where there is hatred,
let me sow love;
Where there is injury, pardon;
Where there is doubt, faith;
Where there is despair, hope;
Where there is darkness, light;
And where there is sadness, joy.

O Divine Master, grant that I may not
so much seek to be consoled as to console;
to be understood as to understand;
to be loved as to love.

For it is in giving that we receive,
it is in pardoning that we are pardoned,
and it is in dying
that we are born to eternal life.

This prayer has come to be such a great source of comfort to me that I say it aloud each morning while driving to the research institute and each evening when returning home, no matter the hour. It settles me down and in the morning brings focus to what my day could be, and at night to what my day has been.

St. Francis tells us that true happiness comes from consoling, understanding and loving our fellow man. His words present clear and precise guidelines for finding increased happiness in our personal lives, for bringing justice to the affairs of men within nations, and for bringing peace among nations. For the last 15 years of my practice (1976-1991), I gave each of my patients, usually when I discharged them from the hospital, a wallet-sized plastic card bearing this prayer. I gave one to Joe the night before his surgery. Most patients kept it in their purse or pocket. Some placed it on their desk, on their bathroom mirror, or on the door of their refrigerator. Many showed me their weathered cards, years later, during their annual follow-up visits to the office. It was clear to me that this card had forged a bond between my patients and St. Francis, and that his message had made a difference in their lives.

I now want you to hear from Joe and nine other patients whose lives were threatened by heart disease and who underwent open-heart surgery, one of them four times. Let them tell you what they have lived through and how these experiences have helped them open their spiritual hearts. Learn from them that happiness comes from reaching out to God and His creation. I hope the wisdom my patients have gained will strike a resonant chord within you. Let your emotions flow with theirs, and allow your spiritual heart to open in synchrony with those of the storytellers as you, for the moment, become one with them.

Figlio Mio

Joseph Forgione

My childhood was bizarre by normal standards because heart disease had its ugly arms around me even in my early life. It happened like this. I was born in Irvington, New Jersey, a suburb of Newark, on November 2, 1947, the first of my Italian immigrant father's two children. He was 16 when he arrived at Ellis Island in 1928. My mother, Anna, a first-generation Italian-American, and my father, Pasquale, met through family friends in 1938, and in 1942, when she was 24 and he 30, they were married. A skilled machinist, my father worked full-time at his trade, and he also ran the family's coal- and ice-delivery business. In my early years we wanted for nothing, but suddenly all that changed.

"My son! My son! *Figlio mio!*" my father sang as he held me, his four-year-old, over his head. He swung me around and around, dancing and laughing, expressing his joy at the unconditional love we shared. I pulled his hair, tugged at his nose and hugged his big, warm neck. I still remember the sweet smell of his after-shave.

Suddenly, without warning, without a kiss or a hug, his eyes rolled upward into his head and he collapsed to the floor with me on top of him, screaming in joy. I had not yet learned to fear—I thought he was playing. I was quickly put to bed, and when I awoke, he was gone. I never felt my father's warmth again, nor saw his face. Many years later I was told he died from a heart attack before he even hit the floor. He was 39.

In those bewildering days before I understood what had really happened, I used to ask, "Mommy, where's Daddy?" I asked over and over. "Mommy, where's Daddy?"

Heartbroken and grief-stricken, she would turn to me and say, "Your daddy went to Texas to be a cowboy."

I was happy about that! Those were the days of the Lone Ranger, Hopalong Cassidy and Roy Rogers. "Yahoo! Mommy, when is Daddy coming home?" I asked that question a thousand times.

"Soon, son, soon," she would reply, "and when he does, he'll bring you a big cowboy hat."

A few days before he died, I vividly remember standing with my father at the foot of the long flight of stairs in our home and hearing him say as he held my hand, "When you're the boss, Joseph, I want you to protect and take care of Mommy and Patricia." It was almost as if he knew that heart disease would soon kill him. That's all I remember of my father. Devastated by his death, my mother rarely spoke about him to me.

I never got my cowboy hat. But the responsibility my father had charged me with at the foot of those stairs was burned into my mind forever.

A short time after my father's death, my paternal grandfather died of a heart attack, after having been an invalid for four years due to a stroke he had the year I was born. My paternal grandmother, in shock after the loss of her husband and son, became so depressed she had to be institutionalized. For reasons I still don't understand, the State of New Jersey seized all our family's assets to pay for her care, leaving my mother, my ten-month-old sister, and me penniless.

We had to move to the tough, inner-city environment of Newark, where my maternal grandparents took us into their home, which my father had bought for them. Both in their 70s, Mary and Anthony Lamatino were poor but sensitive, warm, loving Italian immigrants. I still remember the smells in that house—wonderful aromas of Italian cooking: sausage and peppers, tomato sauce, rosemary chicken, veal cutlets, lasagna, spaghetti and meatballs. Wow! Feast days of the saints were often celebrated for days on end. We had little money, but food for everyone. Many times when I returned home from school, I would find the street vendors' trucks parked outside—the fruit man, bread man, milkman, fish man—and Grandma, who had so little of her own, cooked for all of them. She shared her love and talents with all who walked through her door.

My grandmother also served as a foster mother for orphaned children, some of whom had been left on the doorstep of our parish church. Four of these children lived with us through their teenage years. One of them, Jimmy, was mildly retarded. He was Grandma's favorite, and after she died he lived with Mom, Patricia and me. Now he lives on his own in a condominium that my family provides for him.

Along with us and their foster kids, my grandparents were caring for their son, Tony, who was terminally ill with heart disease. His abdomen would become so huge and bloated from fluid that he could hardly breathe. When he got like that, the doctor would come and drain the fluid off through a huge needle that looked to me as if he had placed a sword in his chest. Draining this fluid made Uncle Tony very weak, though for a few days he could breathe better until his abdomen filled back up. I was horrified by his disease and knew by then that it was the same one that had killed my father, though in a different way. I hated what it was doing to my uncle, and I hated what it had done to my father. After much suffering, Uncle Tony died of a heart attack when I was seven. By then I was terrified of this deadly disease and wondered if it would one day kill me, too. I was beginning to be obsessed with a morbid fear that I would die like my father.

My mother was forced to work long hours at a beauty salon called the House of Glamour. I would often see her crying because of the nightmare we were all experiencing—death all around us, barely enough money, and very little time together.

I often felt lost, without direction—Mom away at work, and Grandma and Grandpa so old they couldn't help. I felt an emptiness and worthlessness. The streets somehow do that to you when you're on your own. Without the love and guidance of a father, I often felt inferior. But I never forgot his prime directive—protect and take care of Mommy and Patricia. This was beginning to translate into "You have to make money to fulfill your commitment."

To help support the family I became a shoeshine boy when I was eight—my first business venture. Though afraid, I worked the rough 16th Avenue bars. All the money I earned shining shoes went into the family cookie jar for food and clothing. But this was not enough. I had to do more and began to buy and sell anything I could "creatively" get my hands on—pillows, fireworks (most of which were illegal), wristwatches and clothing; I became a street vendor.

In the meantime Grandpa's heart was failing. In his day he had been a handsome, strong, Erie-Lackawanna trainman who could do anything, but through the ravages of heart disease, he had been reduced to needing care like a baby. I bathed him, fed him, shaved him and wiped him. Toward the end he had to sit up day and night and fight for air. When I was 14, he died in my arms as I said the "Hail Mary" in his ear. At his funeral, I hugged his cold body as it lay in the casket and mourned my loss, for he had been like a second father to me. His death from heart disease added to my mounting fears of this dreadful scourge and left me feeling alone and frightened.

Grandma, who had heart disease and diabetes, got much worse after Grandpa died, and some of her care became my responsibility. I shampooed her long, silver hair with Oxagon soap and spent all the time I could listening to her stories about our family. Each morning before I left for school, I gave her the insulin injection she required. I always cringed when I did this for fear it would hurt her. When she was near the end, I often stayed by her side all night to try and comfort her as she struggled to breathe. But the night she died I was at my senior prom, and I found it hard to forgive myself for being away. Once again heart disease had struck our family, and my fear escalated still more.

I never felt safe as a kid and grew to become a highly defensive, emotional and intense young man. Heart disease, which I had witnessed throughout my childhood and adolescence, and which had killed my father, uncle, grandfather and grandmother, loomed as a deadly threat to my life. I was now afraid that I would die like my father when I reached 39.

To help Mom, I continued to sell all I could on the streets at night, and I also worked at the House of Glamour after school and on Saturdays, washing women's hair and massaging their feet. Though I was doing all I could to meet my father's request, Mom needed more money to take care of our family, and I looked forward to the day when I could provide it for her.

Soon after I graduated from high school in 1964, I got that chance. I was lucky and got a full-time job paying $52 a week as a clerk for a small paper company in Irvington, a suburb of Newark. I was determined to succeed and worked with such intensity that the owner soon noticed me. A few months later, when one of his seasoned salesmen died suddenly of a heart attack, he offered the route to me, working on commission. This opportunity seemed too good to be true. I quickly accepted, thanked him, and began to work at an intensity that far exceeded that of any of the other salesmen. I pursued every lead that had even the remotest possibility of success and gave my customers quick, efficient, reliable and courteous service. Time and work were not considerations—I wanted to establish myself in the company and be able to take care of my family responsibilities. Within a year I had doubled the size of my customer base and was earning $1,000 a week. This enabled me to take care of Mom and Patricia in a manner that made me feel that I was now doing what my father had requested me to do. Yet despite this early bonanza, I knew that I had to get more education if I was to become a real success.

To do that I enrolled for the fall quarter in the Fairleigh Dickinson University evening school, which began in mid-September 1965. I did not realize that my decision to seek this further education would eventually change my entire subsequent life in marvelous ways I could not foresee at that time.

These events started when I came a little late to my first Western Civilization class and found that there was only one vacant seat left in the entire auditorium, and that seat was next to the most beautiful girl I had ever seen. Just looking at her made my heart race. She had long blonde hair, light blue eyes and striking soft features—Scandinavian. I sat down in that seat and couldn't keep my eyes off her. I heard none of the lecture. My interests were closer at hand. At the end of the class I said, "Hello, my name is Joe Forgione. What's yours?"

She answered quietly, "Jane Thorsen." To my dismay, she didn't wish to continue the conversation and quickly left.

Though we were very different—she was a sweet, lovely, shy, 17-year-old Norwegian country girl and I was a tough, brash, 18-year-old Italian city boy, now with money—I was not to be dissuaded the next day when she said no to my first request for a date. That class took on a new challenge to me— I had to have a date with this girl. Day after day I continued to ask and finally, on October 6, my persistence paid off—she said yes. Shortly afterwards, we went to the University Student Center and visited over a cup of coffee. After a few more dates, I took her home to meet Mom and Patricia. They thought she was very special, and on subsequent visits Mom taught her how to prepare my favorite foods. Over a period of several months, with Mom's guidance and my assessment as the official "taster" of her creations, Jane became a gourmet Italian cook.

Even though I knew from the moment I first sat down next to her that I would one day ask this beautiful girl to marry me, I was also determined to be a financial success before I did so. My measure of adequate success before I could ask her to accept me was to be a millionaire when I proposed. My painful experiences with being poor after my father died undoubtedly contributed to my resolve in this regard.

As I set out to attain that goal, I was driven by thoughts of
my father's death at 39 and by his request that I provide for
the family. I worked all the days and much of most nights. I
wasn't popular in the company with the other salesmen whose
average age was about 55. My success made them jealous. I
was the Catholic street kid they referred to as "the goy from
the gutter." I resented their hostility and their poking fun at
me behind my back—derogatory notes left in my message box
and jokes about me being a "putz." I didn't know what that
meant, but I hated it anyway. The owner was different; he
treated me as if I were his son. He showed me kindness and
consideration and provided me with the opportunity of a lifetime: commission with no ceiling. He said, "Joe, the more
you sell, the more you'll earn. The sky's the limit." There was
a feeling between us, a love that I needed.

His two sons felt very differently. My relationship with
them was the opposite of that with their father. It was the case
of me, the poor street kid who had beaten the odds and
achieved some success, pitted against the rich Wharton-
educated boys who could put every obstacle in my path that
they wanted. I'm sure they stayed up nights thinking of ways
to stop me. Their father, on the other hand, was a just man
who knew what was going on and occasionally would step
forward to help me when his sons got too far out of line. In
spite of their efforts to sabotage my work, I continued to be
successful because I worked harder than they could or would.
Even though I was by then taking complete care of Mom's
and Patricia's expenses, I was nonetheless managing to save
about two thousand dollars a month. But at that rate my pre-
marriage goal of a million dollars seemed very distant.
Though Jane disagreed with my monetary objective, we continued to date as best we could with my unrelenting schedule.

After I'd been at the company for three years, my friend and advocate, the owner, became ill and died. Similar to my grandfather, he had been in many respects also like a second father to me, and I had worked long and hard to make him proud of me. When he had told me, "Good job, Joe," I had felt good through and through. But with him gone, I felt alone and wounded.

Following their father's death, one of his sons became president of the company and the other became chairman of the board. With my protector gone, I was fair game, and they intensified their efforts to drive me out. But I held on selling door to door, one account per call, as many as I could do, day after day. Then it struck me—with the same effort I could sell a hundred accounts with one call if I sold to the head office of chain stores. When I told Mr. President and Mr. Chairman about my idea, they both laughed at me, and Mr. President said, "We're a small, local paper company. How could we ever sell nationally? Stop dreaming of being a big shot. You're suffering from delusions of grandeur."

In 1970 my "delusions" paid off, but not in the manner that I had anticipated. Members of the garment carriers' union who were employed by a large, prestigious department store chain went on strike and set up picket lines in many cities. A senior vice president from their lead store in Newark, whom I had solicited many times before without ever getting an order, called and pleaded with me to deliver packaging materials across the picket line because his current supplier would not. I said, "How much do you want?"

He said, "Everything we use that is paper or cardboard and lots of it."

"Okay!" I said. "You'll have it!"

But Mr. President and Mr. Chairman would have nothing to

do with "my deal." Mr. President said, "If you want this account so bad, go rent a truck and drive it across the picket line yourself." And that's exactly what I did. The order was for $50,000 worth of paper supplies, which was 500 times the average $100 order I usually got. There was big profit in this delivery for my company and a big commission for me, too, even though the order included items we didn't stock. I went all over the city purchasing what else I needed, supervised loading the truck, and drove it myself.

When I approached the loading dock of this huge department store, I panicked! The vice president who had contacted me was pacing outside, and the picketers were walking up and down the sidewalk. I didn't know how to maneuver the truck; I had never driven one before. The loading dock was three stories below ground, and the elevator to take me there looked very narrow. The strikers saw me and headed for the truck. The vice president ran to the elevator, waving frantically for me to come forward. I looked up to heaven and said, "Please, God, help me!" I gritted my teeth, put the truck in gear, clung to the wheel and moved ahead onto the platform with about eight inches to spare on each side. A few seconds later I was safely below ground, where company executives congratulated me for my courage, even though my pants were wet!

Word spread, and from that day forward, this department store chain used my company exclusively and purchased millions of dollars of paper products annually. One by one, other major department store chains called me. By an accident of fate I had developed a one-stop shopping concept—consolidating all paper packaging products used by a retail store into one shipment.

When Mr. President and Mr. Chairman saw this huge surge in their business, they had a change of heart because they recognized that my concept would revolutionize the distribution system of that time. I was now important to them because they had a vision: they would develop my concept and then sell their company for millions. To facilitate this objective they called me "brother," established a national corporate supply division and put me in charge of it, invited me to outings of all types, and convinced me that we were in fact "family."

With the increasing pace of my work, my spare time, which had been short before, completely disappeared. That loss, plus the excitement of major business success and the sense of power that accompanied it, led to Jane and me drifting far apart during the period of 1969-1971. My life became increasingly one-dimensional—sales, sales, and more sales—until the company owned me: body and soul.

With the rapid progress of my division, my commission-based income rose proportionately. This enabled me in 1971 to buy my mother the home of her dreams, in Piscataway, a pleasant community in northern New Jersey. It had five bedrooms, four bathrooms, a spiral staircase and a large fireplace, and we all moved in together—Mom, Patricia and I. This was a big change from my grandparents' old home in the run-down part of Newark, where we had lived for 20 years.

Because I had hit on the right idea for the times and worked feverishly to develop it, my division grew rapidly. The demands of the business never let up and forced me to be away most of the time. But in late 1971, as my millionaire status loomed close ahead, I asked Jane to have dinner with me. After that, one date led to another, and before long we had rediscovered each other and fallen deeply in love. The next year I attained my financial goal and shortly thereafter, at age 25, I asked Jane to marry me. I was elated when she said yes, and thanked God for this greatest blessing of my life. But largely because of my ever-escalating schedule, we were not married until October 6, 1974, in Holy Trinity Church, Lake Telemark, New Jersey. I shall always remember how she looked that day—radiantly beautiful—and she still is. We went to Hawaii for our honeymoon and spent three glorious weeks by ourselves with no pressures of any kind. It was wonderful.

But those peaceful days quickly disappeared on our return, when I plunged into my backed-up, high-pressure schedule, determined now to become richer and more powerful for my bride. I was blind to the fact that she didn't want more money. All she wanted was for me to slow down and enjoy our life together. But I paused only long enough to go and look for a house with her. After looking at several, we bought a new, large colonial on six wooded acres in the rolling Somerset mountains of northern New Jersey, where herds of deer still roam the slopes. After completing this transaction, I returned to my work with even greater intensity than before our marriage.

I strove to widen the client base of my division by working day and night and was very successful. Our accounts soon read like the *Who's Who* of the big department store chains from coast to coast. As my success spread from one state to another, my ego became more and more inflated and progressively consumed whatever was left of my humility. Jane, the only sta-bilizing force remaining in my life, tried her best to calm me down. She would listen to my speeches about the wonders I was creating across the United States, then quietly tell me to ease up because we already had more than enough. But I refused to listen and continued to accelerate even more.

The next year my insane pace began to affect me physically. At first I was just tired by the end of the day. But my fatigue soon got worse, and within weeks I was exhausted by noon. Not long after, I developed throbbing headaches, nosebleeds and eye hemorrhages. I had pushed myself beyond all reason to meet the ever-escalating demands of our burgeoning business empire. My physician was alarmed because my blood pressure (180/120) and my cholesterol (380) were both very elevated. He sent me to a famous medical center in New York City for further diagnosis and treatment. I was there for ten days and given all kinds of tests. Strangely, no one inquired about my lifestyle, which was all wrong at that time—no exercise program, an excessive diet high in fat and red meat, and stress galore. The only thing I didn't do was smoke. The physician who released me said I had essential hypertension, familial hypercholesterolemia, and a stress-related somatic disorder. I was to take Hygroton, a strong diuretic. That was it. Shortly after leaving the hospital, I had to stop taking this drug because it made me so lethargic. Despite this, I was better. Perhaps the rest in the hospital had done me some good.

I went back to work, determined to move the business forward even faster. Within a short time I was once again on a roll and my pace quickened still more. I don't know how, but my body soon adapted to this faster tempo.

The packaging supply market at that time was rapidly expanding, and my company was in increasing demand. I could sense new contracts like a bird dog and tracked them down no matter the distance nor the difficulty. In this mad pursuit I crisscrossed the nation from east to west and from north to south, traveling incessantly from New York to California, from Florida to Illinois, and to most of the states in between. Nothing could stop me. As a result of my vision and efforts, by Christmas of 1976 our company had become the national leader of the packaging supply industry. In the process of all this, my income had soared to over a million a year plus stock options.

While all this business success was happening, my personal life was disintegrating. I was away most of the time and when home, my mind would be preoccupied with the plans for my next financial conquest. I was working 100 hours a week building an empire that was ruining my life. Power and money were not what I thought they would be. Friends were valued according to what they could do for me and the company. I was driven forward by an irrepressible inner force that gnawed at the center of my being and constantly urged me to do more, get more, be more, and never, never stop! But as a consequence I was inwardly becoming ever more desolate. Though I was outwardly gregarious and strong, my spirit was lonely and fragile. I had to be busy constantly to hide from my inner self. I was suffocating my spirit and afraid to confront my essence. My work and its environment were producing sinister changes in me. I had become almost totally self-centered without realizing what was happening. For Jane, the man she had married was becoming only a memory. The real me was now a business machine that used people.

In the process of making more money I had fallen away from the church and ruled God out of my life. I was losing everything that really mattered, but I had grown so spiritually blind I couldn't recognize this. I didn't know what to do as I continued my dismal journey, unable to stop or change course. By then I could no longer even define what I was striving to achieve. In my emotional turmoil I turned in desperation to material objects. I bought everything I could to try to fill the craving and yearning of my empty soul—handmade oriental rugs, 2,000-year-old vases, sports cars, original paintings—but nothing worked until Karen came along.

Karen, our first child, was born on August 7, 1977—a small, red-headed cherub weighing four pounds, eight ounces. She was a wake-up call to what was left of my soul. I responded with joy and, for the moment, began once again to perceive a real purpose in my life: Jane and our baby. But five days after her birth, I had to go to Los Angeles to open a huge warehouse for our extensive and expanding West Coast operation and was gone for ten days. After that, it only got worse. I missed most of Karen's childhood and hated myself for it.

While my financial successes continued to bound forward at an amazing rate, my home life was becoming a progressively worsening nightmare. Jane needed me. My mother wanted to see me. Patricia had problems and was asking for me. Though I tried to help, there was not enough time even to identify their problems, let alone do anything about them. I was failing those who needed me most and deserved my love. I was being wrenched between the company and my family, and the business won out every time.

Mr. President and Mr. Chairman were constantly pushing me to get new, bigger and more lucrative accounts, even though my division was making more than $1 million-a-month profit during the rush seasons and by then accounted for 80 percent of the company's income. Still they weren't satisfied. More, Joe! Get this account or that account. Go! Go! Go! My staff had grown to over 50, supported by about 100 more.

Mom, my wonderful friend and confidante and the center of my life before Jane, was diagnosed during the summer of 1978 to have advanced cancer in her abdomen. When she began to fail, we moved her into our home. Jane and I gave her our bedroom downstairs and we moved upstairs. When I was home, which wasn't often, if Mom needed help, I would sleep in her room to be close. When I was away, Jane took my place beside her.

Throughout that year and most of the next, chemotherapy

and radiation held the tumor in check. But Mom was tired and nauseated most of the time. During the few times when I was home and could take her to the hospital for her treatments, the doctors seemed cold and unsympathetic. I knew they were busy, but a caring word or two from them would have meant so much. We needed support, but they didn't have time.

Then, while my mother's life was ebbing away, God gave us another precious life, a second baby girl, Christine, who was born on October 8, 1979. She, like her sister Karen, was a beautiful baby and I wanted to watch her grow. But as usual, I didn't have enough time for that or the rest of the family because of my impossible schedule. I was on a treadmill that wouldn't stop, and all I could do was try to keep up. More brought more. There was no end to it.

By late 1979, my mother's abdomen had become grotesquely large; the tumor was out of control. Her suffering increased. While her abdomen grew, the rest of her body wasted away. Her once lovely face was drawn and haggard, and all her striking, silver hair was gone, leaving her bald and wizened. I felt her pain like a searing knife thrust into my soul and wished I could endure it for her. When I gave Mom injections of morphine to relieve the terrible pain, I knew but still could not accept that she was dying. A few weeks later she breathed her last and died in my arms as I prayed aloud for her.

Dr. Tom Angelo, a devoted man who cares deeply about his patients, was my mother's internist, and he is mine, too. He knows what it means to be a doctor in the true sense of the word. I'll never forget that he found time to attend her funeral.

After we laid Mom to rest, I threw myself back into work and decided to go all the way and play by Mr. President's and Mr. Chairman's rules. They were pleased. During the next few years the business grew to $100 million in annual sales, led by my dominant division. I was often asked to sign papers and agreements, to cash checks and return the money to the company. I didn't know what happened to it, and I never asked.

The years of 1981 through the summer of 1985 were turbulent times of continuous work, worry, separation from my family, and increasing desperation as I continued to speed toward a destination where I didn't want to go. The only good thing that happened in that period was that God gave us another wonderful life on November 1, 1983: Annie, our third daughter. She had a special sparkle. "A singer from birth," the nursery RN said, bringing her to Jane at two in the morning when she couldn't take her screaming anymore.

In 1983 Mr. President and Mr. Chairman put the company up for sale and took me off commission because I was making too much. They also cut off my stock-option acquisitions, which had grown to 16 percent of the company's value. So much for their father's promise of "The sky's the limit!" They said, "On the date of the sale you'll get millions. Just work harder and get more accounts. Do whatever it takes! Whatever!" I did what they asked and spread our customer base still wider and, in the process, further overwhelmed the competition. But by mid-1985 I needed rest. My mind and body were exhausted. By then I felt pain in my left arm when I went up a flight of stairs, and I couldn't walk a block without getting short of breath. I was now 37. I tried not to think of it, but always looming in the back of my mind was the memory of my father's death and the number 39. I wanted to skip that terrible year.

While I was finding it increasingly difficult to maintain my schedule, Mr. President and Mr. Chairman were carrying on secret negotiations with a national trucking corporation to buy our company for a record price. I was never allowed to read the proposed contract, which was 10 inches thick. Instead, I was asked to accept a 50 percent reduction in salary, continue working for at least five more years, and sign a 10-year agreement not to compete. But to sweeten the terms, they would give me a "quiet gift" of $1.8 million 30 days after the sale. I refused, and the deal fell through.

Mr. President and Mr. Chairman were furious. A few days later they came to my office, entering with a vindictive air that portended retribution, and proceeded to fire me, saying, "Empty your desk, leave your keys, get out and never come back!" Twenty-one years together and the fact that I'd largely built the business meant nothing. Only money counted now. The illusion of family was over; I'd outlived my usefulness. Worse yet, shortly after this, the IRS began an investigation of my business-related activities.

I suspect that Mr. President and Mr. Chairman directed the IRS to me. Ledgers and supporting papers that I needed to prove my innocence had mysteriously disappeared from the corporate office. Without those documents I was largely defenseless. I had been set up for the IRS to indict me for a $6 million income-tax fraud. This libelous charge, unless refuted, would destroy my reputation, take much of what I had, and could even imprison me. This left me no choice but to secure the services of the best tax lawyers in Manhattan and prepare to fight this false accusal to the bitter end even though the chance of overturning the IRS's slanderous accusation was very small. Despite the absence of those essential records, my lawyers were nonetheless able to block the initial attempt of the IRS to indict me.

Mr. President and Mr. Chairman had effectively neutralized me. I was blacklisted and isolated. They had seen to it that I would get nothing from the subsequent sale of the company.

And worst of all, I was considered to be a criminal by the federal government. My business success was gone. I was physically exhausted and spiritually depleted. My 38th birthday brought me ever closer to my feared 39th. Christmas and New Year's were somber occasions. All this was too much for me to bear, and over the course of 1986 I grew progressively more depressed and withdrawn.

I overate, didn't exercise, gained 30 pounds and drank heavily to escape from myself. Overwhelmed by fear and despondency, I took increasing doses of sedatives to sleep, even during the day, and drifted progressively further away from reality. I wanted to die and often hid for long periods in the dark of our recreation room downstairs. I could do nothing right. My depression prevented me from appreciating the joy of Jane and of Karen, Christine and Annie. I was so despairing that I tried several times to take enough pills to sleep forever, but I failed at that, too.

Through the spring and summer and into the fall, the pain in my left arm came on with less and less activity, hurt worse, and lasted longer. When it occurred, I also had trouble breathing. I was fearful that heart disease now had its evil hold on me, but I couldn't give in and admit this to myself. My fright increased and my despair intensified as my shrinking world closed ever tighter around me.

Then, a week before my 39th birthday, the curse that I had feared for so long became stark reality. It was a chilly, gloomy Sunday afternoon in late October with a dark, foreboding sky. A misty rain wet the leaves that had already fallen to the ground. Jane and the children were a few houses up the road at a neighbor's, celebrating a playmate's birthday. Home alone, sitting in my chair in the family room trying to nap, I suddenly felt a bolt of pain flash across the front of my chest and extend down my left arm. At first I wasn't sure if I was awake or dreaming. I was jolted again. Now there was no doubt. I was wide awake, cold, sweating, and experiencing a severe ache over my heart and in my left arm. Fearing that I was about to die like my father had, I reached for the phone and called an ambulance. My family heard its siren echoing across the valley as it sped toward us. When it screeched to a halt in front of our home, they came running.

I remember my family rushing in, and I can still see the look of terror in little Annie's eyes as she watched the emergency technician put an oxygen mask over my face. "Daddy!" she screamed in horror. The older girls were frozen in their tracks. Jane came quickly to my side and held my hand. The attendants moved swiftly, and I was soon in the ambulance being rushed to the hospital where I was admitted to the coronary care unit. After the staff started an IV and gave me special drugs, the pain disappeared. No one told me what was wrong. Instead they said, "We'll talk later." These events left me engulfed by an overpowering fear that now there was disease in my heart that would soon kill me.

The next morning, after I had spent a fitful night, a cardiologist told me I'd have to take a stress test. Though I didn't know what that was, I said okay anyway, and soon an attendant came and wheeled me away. After a technician had attached electrocardiographic leads to both of my arms, to my left leg and across my chest, I was told to stand on the roller platform of the machine and walk in place while it moved. After walking like that for about three minutes, my chest and left arm began to hurt, and I became short of breath. The cardiologist who had been watching the continuous recording of my cardiogram looked concerned, stopped the machine and said, "Lie down." As I stepped off the platform, he gave me a nitroglycerine pill and told me to place it under my tongue. He then said bluntly, "You have very severe coronary heart disease, which has markedly reduced the blood supply to your heart." Just like that: no concern, a cold business fact. My dreaded enemy was here. With those words my fear intensified to near panic. The cardiologist then said, "It will be necessary for you to remain in the hospital for further testing—specifically, an angiogram." When I asked what an angiogram was, he said it was an X ray that would show the surgeon where the blockages were that he would have to bypass.

Shocked by the suggestion of an operation, I said, "What are you talking about? I'm confused. What's blocked? What's this about a surgeon?"

He answered, "I'm certain you'll need open-heart surgery as soon as possible. You'll not be going home." He didn't look at me even once while he was telling me this. I don't trust people who won't look at me.

"What are my chances?" I asked.

"In your case, the risk is higher than average," he said matter-of-factly.

"I want to go home and discuss this with my wife," I said.

"You don't have time to do that. She can come here."

I stayed in the hospital and had another terrible night, tossing and turning until dawn. In the morning I had the angiogram and my worst fears were confirmed. All the arteries to my heart were either blocked or severely narrowed—and not in just one place, but in many. "More typical of someone in their seventh decade of life," the cardiologist said. "You are basically inoperable. In fact, many of your coronary arteries have become like bone. Their walls are so hard that they even show up on your chest X ray."

I was terrified. "Please explain!" I begged him. He was a

cold individual, obviously well trained in medical school to treat disease, but not people. He said impatiently, "Open-heart surgery can't cure you, but it may extend your life for a few years. You must leave immediately for Philadelphia to have it done. I'll contact Dr. X to perform your operation."

"Wait a minute," I said. "This is not a decision I'm going to rush. I'll go home and sort this out in my mind. I must prepare my family for what might happen. And I'll get another opinion, too. Also, I'm going to educate myself about cardio-vascular disease and open-heart surgery."

By now the doctor had become very hostile and said, "When did you graduate from medical school? You are the patient. I am the doctor. Just listen to me and do what I tell you to do!" With that he brushed me off as if he couldn't be bothered with me any longer. He never expressed any feelings of empathy or compassion—only disdain for my insubordination in questioning his authority.

I went home, and the next morning Jane and I naïvely sought the opinion of another cardiologist in the same group. He corroborated precisely what his partner had said and added that the advanced degree of disease in my coronary arteries was extraordinarily rare in a man of my young age.

The following day I went out and bought every book I could find that dealt either with reversing coronary heart disease or treating it by bypass surgery. During the next few days I read all I could, and the more I read the more tense I became. The facts supported what I had been told but did not want to accept: surgery was *necessary!* The increasing pain in my chest made this obvious, too.

The dreaded day, November 2nd, 1986—my 39th birthday—arrived, carrying with it a sense of inescapable doom for me. All but the children, thanks to Jane's protection of them, felt my premonition that I would die during the year from the same disease that had killed my father.

Over the next few days I came to accept that if I were to survive my 39th year, I would have to undergo coronary bypass surgery. I called the surgeon in Philadelphia, who by then had received my coronary angiograms. He said, "I saw your films. We can do it. Your chances of dying in surgery are maybe 5 percent or so, no big deal. Come in and I'll do it for you."

His manner over the phone was so atrocious that I said, "I'd like to meet you before the surgery and discuss my options."

He replied, "You have no options. You don't need to meet me. I'll do your surgery, and we'll talk later."

I said, "Doctor, you don't seem to understand that 5 percent is 100 percent for me if I die. If you're going to cut my chest open, stop my heart and bypass my coronary arteries, I think the least you could do is meet with me before the operation. If you choose not to, I will find someone who will take the time to talk to me. I need emotional support as well as bypass grafts."

"If that's the way you feel," he said, "come to the hospital now and I'll see you tonight, but it will be late."

Jane drove me to Philadelphia and we went to the hospital's admitting department. After filling out endless forms, I was finally taken to my room and told that an attendant would come to shave my body.

When a huge, rough nurse arrived to do this, she was taken aback when I said, "Before you do anything to me, I'd like to meet my surgeon."

"You can't meet your surgeon," she replied. "He's operating now, and I'm here to get you ready for him."

Her response so infuriated me that I shouted in anger, "I'm

going to see the man who's going to operate on my heart before *anyone* touches me, including you!"

Irritated now, the nurse said, "A great many people have their heart surgery done here, and I've never seen anyone act like you. You're irrational. Perhaps you should see a psychiatrist. This is a fine hospital, and we take good care of our patients." With that she strode out of the room, slamming the door behind her so hard it shook the walls.

Jane and I waited, growing more tense and frightened as the evening wore on. Eleven o'clock came, and the surgeon still hadn't arrived. I remember what happened a few minutes later as if it were yesterday. Jane was sitting by the side of the bed nervously holding my hand, when suddenly the door was flung open, whipping the drape in front of it back against the wall. Framed in the doorway was this small, hostile man in his operating gown, the famous surgeon for whom we'd been waiting so long. After glaring at us for a moment, he advanced to the foot of my bed, followed by four large assistants who stood behind him at attention, almost military style.

Then in a loud, surly voice, this Napoleonic figure said condescendingly, "Well, Mr. Forgione, I am Dr. X. I've just reviewed your films again, and they're much worse than I had originally thought. Your chances of dying in surgery are 20 percent—four times the average."

We were stunned, but this man's demeanor was so dreadful that by then I was more angry than scared and asked, "Do you plan to use my internal mammary arteries for the grafts?"

He said, "I can't use them because your disease is so advanced."

"But I've read that they would last longer than grafts made from the veins in my legs."

The famous surgeon by then was furious and screamed,

"You know nothing about this and don't try to tell me what to do!"

Jane was in tears and shaking, and by that time I could barely contain my pent-up rage toward this awful man. This very emotional encounter caused a wave of angina to spread across my chest and forced me to stop and take a nitro pill. While he continued to berate me, the nitro worked quickly and within a minute I could say, "Dr. X, you are frightening my wife. We came here for hope, and you have given us none. You lack judgment in the way you talk to your patients, and I have lost confidence in the way you would perform surgery for me. I am leaving this hospital."

"You mean you are going to walk out on me?"

"Yes, I am."

"But I have you scheduled for 9:00 A.M. My calendar is set."

"Well, I'm sorry to disrupt your calendar, but it's my life we're talking about. I'm going to find a surgeon who is capable of using my internal mammary arteries."

The surgeon, by that point having lost all semblance of control, shouted with contempt permeating each word, "Well, it's your funeral, Forgione; don't blame me!" With that, he and his entourage turned abruptly and departed, leaving Jane and me alone.

Jane didn't want me to leave and said, "Please, Joseph, you need this surgery." I agreed. But not there and not by that man! I signed the "against medical advice" release form, and near 1:00 A.M. we walked out of that hospital, hand-in-hand, fearful but determined.

After returning home I continued to read every conceivable bit of information I could find regarding coronary heart disease, and I researched and consulted the top specialists I could reach regarding coronary bypass surgery. I spoke to doctors at

Baylor University Hospital in Houston, the Cleveland Clinic in Cleveland, Harvard Medical School in Boston, Columbia Presbyterian Hospital in New York City, and the University of Alabama Hospital in Birmingham. They told me what I already knew—that I didn't have much time left.

In December, Dr. Victor Parsonnet, a renowned surgeon at Beth Israel Hospital in Newark, reviewed my films and said something very different: "Mr. Forgione, I cannot perform the surgery that is necessary for you. You need someone who is technically capable of using both of your internal mammary arteries in a special way to restore the blood supply to your *entire* heart, because grafts made from those arteries will function much longer than those made from leg veins. Since you are still a *young* man, this is critical if you are to avoid multiple reoperations during the course of your lifetime. The only person I know of who is capable of doing this for you is Dr. Lester Sauvage of The Hope Heart Institute in Seattle. I've just read an article of his on this subject that was published last week in the *Annals of Thoracic Surgery.* I will call and tell him about your case and say that you'll send him your angiograms by overnight mail."

Though I was encouraged by Dr. Parsonnet's opinion, I was still uncertain what to do because everyone else had been so pessimistic. I procrastinated and mailed my films to Dr. Sauvage two weeks later by regular mail. Seattle seemed so far away. During this period my depression returned and progressed rapidly to become deeper than ever. I became afraid to drive my children anywhere for fear I would suffer a heart attack and have an accident that would kill them. Soon I was afraid even to be near them lest I die in their presence and mark them forever, in the way my father's death had marked me.

Jane was amazingly courageous throughout all of this. She was the eternal optimist who held the family together through the Christmas season and hid my failures and despair from the children. Because of her, they were not even aware of my medical problems.

At that time, God had no place in my life, and I had come to doubt that He even existed. I sank lower and lower until I hit bottom on Sunday afternoon, January 11, 1987, when I took a fifth of liquor and a bottle of pills and went downstairs to the recreation room, locking the door behind me. Jane had taken the children two houses down the road to the birthday party of another one of their playmates. I was now alone and my plans were set. Everyone would believe that I had died of a heart attack and the kids would be traumatized as little as possible.

It was dark and frighteningly quiet. I felt only the pain of life and could no longer perceive its beauty. I sipped away at the Sambuca and took one pill, then another. Hours went by. I was sweating now, afraid. I couldn't feel anything. Then, just as I was about to take all of the remaining pills, the phone rang, breaking the enveloping silence. The shrill noise continued. It wouldn't stop. When I couldn't stand it any longer, I staggered to my feet and picked up the receiver, stumbling as I did so. My mind was swirling. The voice on the other end said, "Mr. Forgione, this is Dr. Lester Sauvage in Seattle, Washington."

I wasn't focusing, but his voice became clearer and louder as if it were coming from inside me, not through the telephone.

He said, "I am calling because Dr. Parsonnet called me about you. I hope that I can help. But first, may I ask if you believe in God?"

As he spoke, a small beam of sunlight broke through the vertical window-blinds, piercing the darkness. And at that very moment, I began to come to my senses and said, "Dr. Sauvage, have you reviewed my films?"

"Yes, but before we talk about that, I have a few questions for you."

He was an unusual man—intense, direct, alarming—and he asked again, "Do you believe in God?"

At that time in my life I wasn't sure. After a moment of stillness, he said, "Mr. Forgione, please answer me."

Dr. Sauvage had no idea who I was, where I was, or what I had been about to do. But somehow he said what I needed to hear. I was immediately attracted to him. His voice, his style, his directness had a unique serenity to it, as if he were reaching out to me from another world.

Then he asked in rapid succession: "Why do you want to live longer? What is happiness to you? What will you do if your life is extended?" These audacious questions spoke to my essence and cut to the center of my being.

I wanted to know about his surgical skill and whether he was capable of helping me, and he wanted to know why I wanted to live longer. At that time I didn't know that Dr. Parsonnet had told Dr. Sauvage of my tremendous fear and anxiety. Perhaps because of this, he wouldn't answer any of my questions until I answered his. This made me feel as if I were talking to a priest, like I was going to confession. But somehow his direct approach had jarred me to the depths of my soul and dispelled all the desire that I'd had but a few minutes before to end my life.

I responded to his questions from my heart, as from a voice deep within me, and said, "Dr. Sauvage, I want to live for my family. I don't want my children to grow up without a father like I did. I want to be the best father I can be. I want to be the best husband I can be. And I must be alive to do that. I want to make up for what I haven't done. I want to be a part of their lives and help guide them through the obstacles they'll face. I'll live my life differently if I'm given the chance."

I had dug deep into my soul to answer him and for the first time in a long time, I felt good about something.

My answer seemed to make Dr. Sauvage feel good, too. He said, now softly, "Joe, nobody meets by accident. We have met for a purpose. You need the surgery. God wants you to live and for me to help you. Come to Seattle."

For several days after that I was confused and uncertain. I wondered at times if this unusual man really existed and, if he did, if he had really called me. Was I imagining this? Were my senses playing tricks on me? After all, I had been drinking heavily and taking pills to kill myself when his call came.

Dr. Sauvage must have intuited my turbulent mental state because he didn't let that one phone call be the end of our relationship. He contacted me several more times over the next few weeks, calling after he had finished his last operation in the evening to reach me near midnight Eastern time. Without those calls I would have never been sure that he had called me that Sunday afternoon, and I would most certainly have never gone to Seattle to have surgery.

Nonetheless, fear still crippled me. The thought of anyone, even Dr. Sauvage, stopping my heart terrified me. Could he bring me back after what so many doctors had told me? This haunting question kept me from making the decision to move ahead.

But the logic of those late-night discussions and my worsening angina helped me realize that if I wanted to live, I couldn't continue to vacillate in indecision. My time was running out. Though agonizingly difficult, I finally made the decision during the first week of February to go to Seattle and have Dr.

Sauvage perform my surgery. Even so, I was still very apprehensive because I knew there was a significant chance that I wouldn't survive the operation. Since I was concerned about what would happen to Jane and the children if I were to die 3,000 miles from home, I asked her parents to accompany us so that they could help and comfort her in the event she had to take me home in a casket.

We prepared to leave for Seattle three times—Jane, the children, her parents and me. The first two times they were all in the van waiting for me to get in so we could go to the airport. But I became so frightened that I couldn't get in to start the trip across the continent to an unknown destiny. Though I was ashamed of my fear, I simply couldn't take that last step. On both occasions Jane quietly said, "That's all right, Joseph. We'll go another day when you feel better." Inwardly she must have been completely distraught with me, but she never let on. There's no way I could have gained the courage to make that journey without her love, understanding and patience. Those last-minute cancellations were not only hard on my family, they were also upsetting to Dr. Sauvage's staff, who had to rearrange his surgery schedule both times.

Finally, on Wednesday, February 25, 1987, I was able to summon sufficient inner strength to get in the van. We went to the Newark airport, where we left for Seattle, with a stop in Chicago. As we sped across the country, my mind was beset with dread, even when I dozed off. Then, when the pilot announced that we were beginning our descent into Seattle, I held Jane's hand and looked across the aisle at our children, who thought they were going on a vacation. My eyes filled with tears and my throat choked up as I wondered if I would be with them on their return flight. At that very moment I looked out the window and saw majestic, snow-covered Mt.

Rainier, towering over 14,000 feet into the sky. This colossus of nature looked so close and beautiful that I wondered if it was an omen that eternity was near for me.

A few minutes later the pilot made a smooth landing and though I felt a little better, I was still on edge and engulfed by a foreboding state of mind. Though I was intensely anxious to meet Dr. Sauvage at his office the next day, a part of me was afraid to do so. Who was this man who had confronted me in such a forceful way at a time when I had been about to take my life?

To my utter surprise, when we disembarked, Dr. Sauvage was there in his surgical scrub suit to meet us, with two of his staff from The Hope Heart Institute—his medical artist, Trese Rand, and his executive assistant, Joan Strand. He knew it was me, and I knew it was him. His first words to me were, "Joe, I'm glad you're here. I'm confident you'll do fine." I thought how different this was from my meeting with Dr. X in Philadelphia, and I felt much better.

Dr. Sauvage was intense and concerned but friendly, and he looked straight at me when he spoke. He made us feel at home. Then he explained that he had to get back to the surgery, and left us in the care of his staff.

After we had collected our luggage, I was reassured by the gentle, efficient way they moved us along and took us to our accommodations. His staff had arranged for my whole family—Jane, me, the kids and my in-laws—to stay in a pleasant apartment near the hospital. Trese had decorated the children's room with cartoons and balloons, and had crayons and clay for them to play with. Joan had bouquets of flowers in the living room to brighten the atmosphere and had filled the refrigerator with food. They succeeded in making our apartment a home away from home.

The next afternoon I went to Dr. Sauvage's office, where he took my medical history, examined me, and then reviewed my angiograms with me. Then we talked about the plan for my total care and our respective responsibilities in this comprehensive program. He told me that I had made good progress in getting my fear under control and he felt I was now ready to move ahead. He emphasized that we were partners in a carefully drawn-up strategy to take care of the whole me, not just my coronary arteries. He said that, of course, he had the responsibility to perform the technical aspects of my surgery to perfection while I was asleep. But after I left the hospital I had the responsibility to live my life in such a way that the chemistry of my body would be optimally regulated to assure that the benefits achieved by my operation would be long-lasting. He said that together and with God's help, we could do what had to be done to defeat the disease process in my heart that was threatening my life. He made me realize that I was an important part of the team that was working to save me. His confidence was infectious.

Next, we briefly reviewed the importance of a happy life to my health. He didn't spend much time on that aspect of my care because we had spoken in depth of this in our several telephone conversations. At that point he gave me an autographed copy of his book *The Lifelines Within Us* for my family and me to read. He said everything we had talked about and much more was in this illustrated volume. He wrote this book to tell his patients and their families how cardiovascular disease can be diagnosed, treated and prevented. In it he also talks about generic spirituality. I read parts of this book that evening and gained some reassurance, but I was still fearful. I tried to calm my mind by focusing on positive things, like going home with my family.

The next morning I was admitted to the Providence Medical Center, where I began a long day of preparation for my operation. After having my blood studies, cardiograms and X rays, I received a phone call in the mid-afternoon of that already stressful day from one of my lawyers in Manhattan, telling me that the IRS was preparing to indict me when I returned home. My stress level went through the ceiling. It's a wonder that I didn't have a heart attack on the spot.

Fortunately for me, Dr. Sauvage surrounds himself with people who care, because I needed help after that message. One of these people was Kevin Walsh, a man in his early 50s who was a body-shaver for the surgery department. What a different person he was from that nurse in Philadelphia! Friendly, talking easily in the late afternoon, he was in no apparent rush, but he wasted no time either.

"I'm going to shave your body, but it won't hurt," he said. "It'll be easy. I'll make you comfortable and cover up all the areas we're not working on."

He was very tender. He told me stories as he was shaving my body. One was very special. He said, "You know, when you wake up after surgery, the first thing you'll remember is the last thought you had on your mind when you drifted off to sleep with the anesthetic. So why not go to sleep with pleasing thoughts and wake up to them? When you start to drift away, imagine yourself on a beautiful warm beach in the Caribbean with no one else in sight. You are walking on the cool, wet sand at the edge of the water with the gentle waves rhythmically cresting over your feet and then receding. You are bathed by the warm glow of the morning sun on your back as you continue walking toward the distant horizon, which is sprinkled with wispy white clouds to the west. You are enjoying the relaxing beauty of the sea, the beach, the sky, and of life itself. You will walk until you become tired, and then you will lie down under the protective shade of a grove of tall palm trees and drift off to a peaceful sleep while Dr. Sauvage does your operation. After a time, you will awaken refreshed and continue walking down that beach, enjoying all that you did before you slept."

After Kevin finished and prepared to leave, I thanked him. He had been efficient and loving at the same time. He was a professional at his job and much more besides. Though I was still nervous, pent up and tense, he had helped me.

Soon it was time for dinner, and my family joined me. The children watched me take a bite of this and that, and said little. They sensed my fear, even Annie. After the nurse's aide took my tray, the children kissed me good-bye, one by one. Perhaps for the last time. After the children, my in-laws said goodbye, and finally, Jane. As I kissed her, I whispered, "I love you my darling, now and forever," and thought back to that evening of long ago when we had first met.

I didn't want to let them go. After they left the room, I cried like a person in mourning because I feared I would never see them again.

Shortly afterward, my anesthesiologist, Dr. Tim DeCook, came to see me. After carefully reviewing my case, he explained everything that he would do for me in surgery. Tim was a master of the pun and the one-liner and said he was from Iowa, where the tall corn grows. He made me smile and that helped reduce my tension.

Later, nurses from the intensive care unit and a respiratory therapist stopped by to check me over and give instructions for the next day. They also wanted to make sure I was okay and answer any last-minute questions I might have.

Much later in the evening, when all was quiet, Dr. Sauvage

came in; he had been in surgery all day. His style was different now. He handed me a little card that said "Prayer of St. Francis" and invited me to read it with him. After we had done that, he said, as he turned to leave, "I am confident that God will bless our work for you."

After he left I read that prayer over and over. The night was long. I only dozed a little, and mostly just waited, while the hands of the large clock on the wall moved relentlessly toward my morning deadline of 6:30, when I would be taken to the surgery. But somehow I now felt good—comforted and peaceful—prepared for life and prepared for death, at God's discretion. I could now accept His will. I'll never know for sure, but I believe St. Francis made the difference. At 5:00 I was given the sedative Tim had ordered for me, and this further eased any tension that remained.

I dozed briefly and then awakened as the time for my departure approached. I knew Saturday was Kevin's day off, but he opened the door and wheeled his transport cart in beside my bed and helped me get on it.

"I didn't expect to see you today," I said.

"I didn't have anything else to do, so I came in to remind you to think of the beach."

On the way to surgery, Kevin told me more stories. I looked up at his badge. It said "Medical Transport," which didn't in any way describe his gentle, deeply spiritual nature. He touched my life with his love.

Kevin wheeled me into Dr. Sauvage's spacious surgery, helped me onto the operating table, and told me to start my walk down the beach. Tim quickly put a tube in the artery at my left wrist, another in the vein in the right side of my neck, and still another in a vein in my right forearm. Then he told me I would soon take a pleasant nap. I asked God's help and continued walking down Kevin's beach, and was soon fast asleep in the shade of the palm trees.

Though I had read about all aspects of open-heart surgery, something happened during my operation that I had not read about. Something happened. I remember so vividly, even today. Before I woke up, while I was being operated on, I remember feeling very light, warm and peaceful. It was a comfortable, sweet, wonderful, almost indescribable feeling—a seductive peace. I was floating, surrounded by beautiful soft colors of blue, green, yellow and orange. No turmoil, no stress or anxiety, no desire to be anyplace but there, floating. I felt my mother and father's presence and the feeling of security they provided so long ago. I could reach out and touch them. I was not attached to my body. I felt free from the confines of life. There was no time, no urgency, no pressures. I was near Jane and the children and my parents all at the same time. The past and the present were one. Just harmony with God. God, to me, was that experience—an experience of ecstasy.

The next thing I felt was being pulled down, almost dragged back into my body. I remember hearing Dr. Sauvage saying, "Joe! Joe! Wake up! Wake up, Joe! Wiggle your toes!" I did. The medical records show I woke up with a start. Tim had timed my anesthetic perfectly, so that I would wake up quickly. He told me that I almost jumped off the operating table.

I am convinced that I experienced God during my surgery. The same God whom we call by different names in different religions. The God of nature, peace, light and beauty. The God of eternity. What a wonderful, happy future eternity can be for all of us. I believe I experienced a moment of it. Being one with God is being one with eternity.

Dr. Sauvage used both of my internal mammary arteries,

which he freed from inside the front of my chest, to bypass five of my blocked coronary arteries, and he also removed the cholesterol and calcific material that blocked two other important arteries so that my new blood supply could reach them, too. After being on the heart-lung machine for four hours, I developed diffuse oozing from all areas of my wound. Dr. Sauvage kept me in surgery until the bleeding stopped, which required an additional eight hours. Then he closed my wound and took me to the cardiac intensive care unit, where Tim soon removed the breathing tube from my windpipe so I could talk. Dr. Sauvage then brought Jane in to see me, and after we had kissed I went to sleep and continued walking on Kevin's beach.

I woke up about 4:00 A.M. on Sunday and saw that Dr. Sauvage was asleep in a reclining chair next to my bed. The nurses said he often slept like that, staying near his patients until he knew they were okay. Before long, he awoke and asked, "How do you feel?"

I said, "I want to take a shower, wash my hair and see my family."

"Well, I'll help you," he said, and proceeded to wash my hair with a warm moist towel he placed over my head. Then he dried my hair with a new towel, gave my scalp an invigorating massage, and lastly, combed my hair. This "treatment" made me feel and look much better. I could tell he had done this many times before and that he enjoyed doing it. He wasn't too big or important to perform such services for his patients.

Later in the morning, Dr. Sauvage allowed Jane to bring our three daughters in to see me. He closed the door to my room and said, "Enjoy!" Annie jumped on the bed and then onto my stomach. Karen and Christine touched and pulled at the wires and tubes, setting off every alarm in the unit. We laughed! (The nurses didn't.)

Dr. Sauvage knew my family would renew me, and they did. I walked, climbed stairs, ate, played with my children and recovered so fast that he released me on the sixth day. Meanwhile, he had members of his staff chauffeuring my children around Seattle—to the zoo, the aquarium, the movies, the amusement park—so that they thought the entire time they were in Seattle was a holiday. They still recall those days as a happy memory.

Before I left the hospital, Dr. Sauvage said: "Joe, although I have provided you with the best of surgical care, you now need the best of medical care, because you are not like the average patient with coronary heart disease. Your problem is much more severe. You have an inherited abnormality of your liver that prevents it from removing cholesterol from your blood. You need to know more than I can teach you. I want you to call Dr. Dean Ornish in San Francisco when you get home. He is doing work that is vitally important to your longevity, and you must follow his instructions to the letter in order to live a long and full life."

Dr. Sauvage came to the apartment the night before we left for home, and after he had checked me over thoroughly, we spoke at length about the life that lay ahead of me. I asked him, "What can I do for you?"

He said, "Joe, God wants you to live for a reason. Go out and find that reason and make a difference in our world."

We left for home the next morning, two weeks after we had come to Seattle. It had been a time of fear and eventual triumph for me, both spiritually and physically. It was the beginning of my new life. For Jane and her parents it had been a time of anguish followed by thanksgiving. For our children it had been a time of joy.

Once home I convalesced rapidly, gaining strength by the

day. My spirits were bolstered when my lawyers informed me two weeks after we had returned that they had again been able to block the IRS's attempt to indict me. I thanked God for this and my innumerable other blessings.

A few weeks later it was time for me to call Dr. Ornish. When I reached him, he answered his own phone! "Call me Dean," he said, and explained in detail the lifestyle-modification program he had developed for the reversal of coronary heart disease. Then he asked if I would like to attend his ten-day seminar in Berkeley, California, which was scheduled to begin in early May. At that time, my cholesterol was 468 and my answer was a resounding "Yes!"

That seminar was a great experience in which Dean taught us the importance of diet, exercise, stress management, yoga and meditation. Because my liver is unable to remove cholesterol from my blood, I needed to become a vegan (an extreme vegetarian who eats nothing of animal origin: no meat, fish, milk, eggs or even honey). After a life of meat-eating, I realized that this was going to be an enormous change for me. Dean's dietary staff taught us how to properly prepare this stringent diet.

While I was at Berkeley, all my meals—breakfast, lunch, and dinner—were prepared according to the demanding diet that Dean had designed to reverse plaque formation, or at least stop its progression, in the arteries of the heart and elsewhere in the body. Since then, the real burden in our household has been on Jane, who has had to become a personal Ornish-type dietitian for me. At first I wondered if I could live this way, but after a couple of months I had to admit that eating this way could still be a pleasure, thanks to Jane's culinary skills.

At that time, Dean was involved in testing the extent to which his program could stop or even reverse coronary heart disease. In 1990, the highly respected English medical journal *The Lancet* published his early findings, which showed that progression was stopped in most patients and that limited regression was achieved in a few. This article was the first recognition by "mainstream" medicine of Dean's pioneering work, which now is widely acknowledged.

Since my operation, I've made progress in perceiving my life as an eternal gift from God. I've also made progress in gaining a proper perspective of earthly life as only the beginning of my existence and in appreciating that the death of my body is not the end of me. I'm making progress in accepting that when this transition occurs does not really matter, be it tomorrow, next year, or 50 years from now. What matters is that I accept this decisive moment as part of my continuing spiritual life. I no longer fear the time of my physical death the way I once did. Instead, I now envision that this moment can be the portal into an eternity of infinite joy with my Creator.

In these years following my surgery, I have looked for opportunities to help the poor in the general region where we live. One such an opportunity presented itself when the priest in charge of a shelter for the homeless in a nearby town asked me to join its board of directors. The board was made up of doctors, lawyers and businesspeople from the community who would write federal and state grant requests for money to fund the shelter and then decide what was best for the homeless to eat and how many could sleep there at one time.

I soon became bored with this executive approach and went into the shelter and started looking at the homeless. What I had suspected was true. There was great potential in these unfortunate people. Once convinced of this, I decided to try a different approach. I organized them into a work force and started a construction company to work on inner-city projects.

Many eventually learned a trade and became proud of themselves. This experience helped me realize that the most effective charity is to help people help themselves.

I have won with some and lost with others. But the important thing is that I have not given up. God only asks that we do our best. I get discouraged sometimes; then I read St. Francis's prayer, and I'm ready to go again.

A precious moment for our family occurred on September 28, 1988, when Jane gave birth to little Joey. He wouldn't be here if I hadn't had my surgery. Dr. Sauvage asked me to live my life to the fullest and not act as if I were going to die in a year or two. This birth of our fourth child, our son, is living testimony to my renewed beliefs and rediscovered spirituality. Joey's mere presence is a constant reminder to me of the great goodness of life.

One of the most gratifying experiences of my life occurred on May 15, 1992, when I was privileged to be one of several people commenting on Dr. Sauvage's life and work at a community banquet in his honor, at which he was to receive the Seattle First Citizen Award for his many contributions to mankind. Other speakers included Dr. C. Rollins Hanlon, former professor of surgery at St. Louis University and later director general of the American College of Surgeons for 14 years; Dr. Paul Brand, a famous scientist and medical missionary; Dr. William Hutchinson, founder of the renowned Fred Hutchinson Cancer Research Institute; and the Reverend Jeff Smith, the "Frugal Gourmet" of TV and book fame, another of Dr. Sauvage's patients.

When I spoke, I said from my heart what this dedicated and happy man means to me—how he had helped me learn the lesson of spiritual love, which in many ways has been even more important to me than the miracle he performed for my physical heart. Toward the end of my tribute I shared my secret, which I had never revealed to anyone before, including Dr. Sauvage that I had been in the process of committing suicide when he first called me. I cried when I told this story of my life, and felt as if a heavy weight had been lifted from my soul when I finished. In closing, I surprised the audience by lifting my three-year-old son Joey (whom they had not been able to see until that very moment) high above my head and then, as I looked toward heaven, proclaiming in thanks to God and in remembrance of my father, "My son! My son! *Figlio mio!*"

I have recently had more good news—my long-running encounter with the IRS is over. After finally acknowledging that they had only a minor case against me, we settled out of court for a small sum, clearing my name at last.

It is now nine years since my surgery, and I'm continuing to do well. I run six miles each morning, adhere to the same strict diet, and follow the rest of Dean Ornish's demanding program, too. But despite this and the powerful medications I take, my cholesterol is slowly going up again. I don't know what lies ahead, but I have today and that's what counts. I have Jane, and we have Karen, Christine, Anne and Joey.

For many years I was lost and unhappy, but through the grace of God, I have found my way back to peace and joy and am thankful for each moment of every day. I have come to know that my happiness in this world comes from being the best husband and father I can be and helping all those outside my family that I can to the full extent of my capabilities. In this process I have been blessed beyond measure, and I thank God for the gift of His love and for the opportunity to serve Him through all that I can do in each day of the rest of my life.

Comments by Dr. Sauvage

I was shocked by what Joe revealed at the First Citizen's banquet about his suicide attempt, and I cried, too. There's no denying that I felt acutely the responsibility of caring for him. I dreaded the thought that I might have to bring news to Jane that he had died in the surgery. My only recourse was to do what I did for all my patients—ask God for help and do my best.

The extensive disease in Joe's coronary arteries made suturing grafts to them exceedingly difficult. The walls of many of his vessels were like bone, and some of the needles broke when I tried to force them through the hardened tissues. While my team and I worked, I prayed that his heart would start up when we were finished. I breathed a sigh of relief when it did and thanked God that the beat was true and powerful due to its new blood supply.

Early in our discussions I told Joe that surgery could not cure the underlying biochemical abnormalities that had caused the blockages to develop in his coronary arteries. I emphasized that his bypass grafts could only compensate for the obstructions that were present at the time of his operation. Our goal from the time of his surgery has been to prevent the hardening process from progressing and causing more blockages to form, which could again deprive his heart of its vital blood supply. Understanding this strategy is important for all patients who must have bypass surgery. For Joe it is *critical*. He *must* do everything that is possible each day to protect his heart by diet, exercise and medications in order to preserve the benefits achieved by his surgery.

In addition to these medical measures, Joe has made and is continuing to make great inner progress through prayer, meditation, and work with the homeless and forgotten. Today, through the synergism of his combined programs of medical and spiritual care, he is a happy man who I believe will live to see his children's children.

Who Would Take Care of Them?

Julia Boutwell

I'm now 78 and have lived here in this little house for 20 years. There's no doubt I would be lost without my dog, Bennie, and my cats, Sam and Stinker. But with the little income I have, I need to watch every penny to be able to take care of them. When my medicines, rent, utilities, clothes and a few other things are paid for, we've only got six dollars a day left to live on. We manage to eat okay, but I have to be careful or there'll be nothing left for us toward the end of the month. Last month I had a dime left over, and I saved it.

My life hasn't been easy, but I'm happier now than I've ever been. This is so even though my heart nearly killed me five years ago. I was a mess.

I got a bad start in life, being born the middle sister of three on a small farm near the little town of Grandview, Washington, on November 9, 1918. My dad wanted a son but got me instead, and he was never happy about that. He treated me like a boy and started me milking the cows when I was five and working in the fields when I was seven. To this day I can't stand milk—probably because I never liked those bossy old Holsteins. My father had a terrible temper and took it out on me. Once, when I was 12, he knocked me out because I was an hour late getting home. I didn't stick around a whole bunch after that. My first job after leaving home was as a soda jerk. Following that I did whatever I could find.

As time passed I hoped I'd meet the right man. I did, on a blind date in 1936, but at first I didn't realize that Reuben was the one. He was a big, handsome, stubborn German, a building contractor with curly black hair who didn't excite me when we first met. After all, he was ten years older than me and seemed too set in his ways. But he was crazy about me and decided I was his from the very moment he set eyes on me. On our second date he said, "I'm going to marry you." And I told him, "You're nuts." Well, the more we went together, the more I found we had in common, and before long I fell in love with him and said, "Yes." We were married a few months later, and while Reuben was alive, I never wanted for anything again. When I close my eyes I can still see him and our beautiful eight-room home.

We had two children, Joyce in 1937, and Damon in 1947. Reuben was good to me, and for 20 years we had a happy life together. Then suddenly all that changed in December of 1956. Reuben had suffered from bad arthritis for years and took cortisone to relieve the pain. But this drug caused a big ulcer in his stomach that bled so much the doctor had to cut it out to stop the bleeding. Five days later, on Christmas, he was doing fine, and we were all thankful. I'd just left his room to get a drink of water when a voice from above told me, "Julia, I'm taking Reuben home." I ran back to his room as fast as I could, but it was too late. He had just died of a massive blood clot to his lungs. The doctor said later that the clot came from the veins in one of his legs and traveled to his lungs where it blocked the passage of blood and killed him. For years after that shock, I couldn't sit down to Christmas dinner, because all I could see was Reuben lying in bed with his mouth open, gasping for air.

Two months after Reuben was buried, I went to work as a nurse's aide at the Hillcrest Nursing Home in Grandview, under Old Lady Belt, and worked there for 13 years until I married my second husband, Al, in late 1969. He was 50 and I was 51. His son and mine had arranged a date for us, and we hit it off from the first. Before we knew what had happened, we were in love and talking marriage. It still seems amazing to me that we were married only a few months after we first met.

Al was a staff sergeant in the army and was stationed at the Yakima firing range. His first wife had died in 1960 following heart surgery at the big army hospital in San Francisco. Of course, after our marriage I left Grandview and moved to Yakima with him.

Al was the biggest man I'd ever seen. We were a strange-looking couple—like Mutt and Jeff. He was 6 feet, 3 inches and I was 4 feet, 11 inches. When I'd get mad at him, I'd hop up on a chair and let him have it. Al never touched a drop of liquor while we were going together, but he made up for it after we were married. When he drank too much, he'd get happy as a lark. If he would've behaved himself, he could've been a captain. But Al liked his beer too much—did he ever!

I think that's what finally did him in. But through all his drinking, he never laid a hand on me.

It's hard for me to think back to his fatal heart attack, which happened after we'd been married for seven years. He was struck down without warning on September 13, 1976, when he was seized with terrible pressure in his chest and couldn't breathe. I rushed him to the hospital, but he died three days later, despite everything the doctors could do. I sat beside his bed for those three days, praying that he'd live.

I didn't go back to work after Al died. He left me his pension, and one month after I buried him I rented this little three-room house and have lived here in West Yakima with my pets ever since. When I moved here, I was 58 and knew things weren't going to get any better for me. I knew that I'd have to make do with what I had. I was alone and wanted to stay here until I died. Yeah, you start to look at things differently when you're alone. It took me awhile to adjust. You have to find yourself. I've been happy here. I don't know how to put it, really, but it's like I told a friend of mine when she said, "Don't you get lonesome?" and I said, "No, I don't get lonesome. I'm not alone. My Boss is with me all the time. God is my Boss."

Al got a kitten for me right after we were married, and I named her Christy. She moved here with me in 1976 and ruled the house. She *ruled* the place. Did she ever! Christy died four years ago, with her paw in my hand. I cried—oh, did I cry—when she went. She'd been part of me for 23 years. I buried her in the backyard under the apricot tree, and I tell you, it was like burying one of my children. I cried all day and was sad for weeks. Sometimes it seems she's still here, curled up on the couch. It's a good thing I had Bennie, my cockapoo, and Sam, my Siamese, when Christy died. I couldn't have managed alone.

I got along okay in my own little world until my heart started to go bad about eight years ago—of course, I didn't know it was my heart. I'd never gone to a doctor. Besides, I couldn't anyway; they cost too much. I didn't know what was wrong and kept it to myself. I didn't tell Damon, who lived in Yakima, or Joyce, who lived in Seattle. I suppose they wondered what was wrong with me, but I didn't say anything. The front of my chest would hurt when I walked—right in the middle. Sometimes I'd pound it, but it didn't do any good.

At first this pain would only come on after I'd walked two or three miles, but soon the burning and the pressure got worse, came on sooner and lasted longer. This was hard on all of us because we didn't eat unless I could walk to the grocery store to get our food. I've never had a car and couldn't drive one if I did. They're way out of my league. Cabs are, too, because they cost a mint. And I don't ride the city buses because the steps are too steep for my short legs. Before long I could barely cross the street. If I was crossing and a car was coming, I couldn't move faster. It just had to stop and wait for me.

I lost my appetite. Nothing had any taste. I couldn't eat; it was too much of an effort. I wanted to sleep. In the last year before my surgery I lost 60 pounds. Even though I couldn't eat, I had to get food for Bennie, Sam and Christy. I couldn't let them starve. I *had* to get to the store, though there were many times when I thought I'd never make those four blocks to get there and back.

In the last months I had so much trouble breathing when I tried to lie down that I had to prop myself up on a big pile of pillows to be able to breathe and get any sleep. If I didn't, I'd choke. By then I couldn't walk 50 feet without my chest hurting so much and my breath getting so short that I'd have to stop and hold on to whatever was near. I knew that something terrible was about to happen, but I didn't know what to do. Going to the store became almost impossible. I could barely think and was confused most of the time. I felt like hell and vaguely knew that I was near the end of my rope.

I tried to hide my condition from Damon—told him I was on a diet. But when I got so weak that I couldn't answer the phone, he figured me out. One day in late August he came over and found me curled up on my Hide-A-Bed, nearly unconscious. At first he thought I was dead. I must have been nearly gone, or I would never have allowed him to take me to the hospital. When he got me there, Dr. Beck saw me in the emergency room and admitted me straight to the intensive care unit, where Dr. Krueger, the heart specialist, took over.

The medicines he prescribed worked, and after several days I felt a little better. I wanted out of that place, but instead Dr. Krueger put dye in my veins and did a special study of my heart. He told me that both of the valves on the left side of my heart were terrible, and that two of my three main coronary arteries were blocked. He said I needed surgery, but it was too risky. I didn't want an operation, I wanted to go home. My neighbor was taking care of Bennie and the cats. Dr. Krueger said I wasn't ready to go. I didn't like that, but I couldn't do a damn thing about it.

After what seemed like forever, he must have decided that I was as good as I was going to get. I really wasn't much better, but I sure wasn't going to tell him that when he finally said, "I've done all I can. Let's see how you do at home."

I said, "It's about time."

I was glad to get home and take care of my pets again, even though I was still far from well. But I was enough better that I could go to the store and get our food.

I was able to hold out for about three months. Christmas

was nothing. Then I got much worse, and on the fourth of January I became so weak and short of breath that Dr. Krueger had to put me back in the hospital and give me more medicines. When I was beginning to feel a little stronger, he told me, "You'll have to have surgery, or you'll die."

I was frightened. To tell you the truth, I was scared spitless. The doctors talked mostly to Joyce, who'd come over from Seattle. They'd talk right in front of me. I didn't understand the details, but I knew it was bad.

Dr. Krueger made an appointment for me to see Dr. Sauvage in Seattle. He said if anyone could fix my heart, he could. When Joyce took me to see him, I was so scared that if he'd said "boo," I would've jumped out the window. I wasn't afraid of the surgery, I was afraid he was going to tell me that he couldn't do it.

He could tell I was petrified. Then something happened. I don't know what it was, but his dark brown eyes did it for me. All at once, I wasn't frightened anymore. He told me he'd do my surgery two days later. He asked me why I wanted to live longer, and I told him that my pets needed me. He said that was an excellent reason, and I felt good.

I said the Lord's Prayer the night before surgery and prayed for God to guide Dr. Sauvage's hands. I told God that if He wanted to take me home in surgery, it was okay, but if my work here on earth wasn't done, to give me more time to finish it. I believe I heard Him answer, "Don't worry, Julia, everything is going to be all right. You're a fighter." When Dr. Sauvage came in around midnight, he said: "I am confident God will bless our work for you." I believed him and went to sleep.

I don't remember anything about the next four days. Then I came to, walking down the hall with a nurse on each side of me. I looked at them and said, "Why in the world are we doing this?" They said, "Doctor's orders. We have to walk you." I said, "Let me try it alone." So they let loose of me, and I took two steps and nearly fell on my face. But as I started to fall, they grabbed my arms to hold me up and took me back to my room.

Dr. Sauvage replaced my two heart valves that were too small and couldn't close, and placed two grafts to bring more blood supply to my heart. He told me that my big artery and my valves were so full of calcium that they were like rock. He could hardly cut through them, and at one point he wondered if he could even finish my operation. I was on the heart-lung machine for seven hours. But after that walk down the hall, I did fine and gained strength rapidly.

When Dr. Sauvage told me I could go home ten days after my operation, I was so happy that I couldn't restrain myself. I asked him to bend over and when he did, I put my arms around his neck and kissed him on the cheek. After that we talked about the years that lay ahead of me. He also gave me the Prayer of St. Francis of Assisi and suggested that reading it would help me see things right when the going got tough.

As soon as I got home, Bennie, Sam and even old Christy ran across the street from my neighbor's and barked and meowed up a storm, and then they crowded around my feet to get in the house when Joyce opened the door. Were they ever happy to see me! I tell you, I never got so much attention in my life. I was sure happy to see them, too. We were all happy to get back into our little house—it's home to us. I missed my furry friends, and they missed me.

Dr. Sauvage had insisted that someone needed to be with me for at least the first two weeks I was home. I fooled him. After Joyce took me home, I shooed her away two days later. I could take care of myself.

The winter was long and cold, but we got along. Except for the groceries, I didn't go out for the next month because of the snow and ice. No broken hip for me because that would have meant a nursing home and no one to take care of them. The electric heater felt so good on those frigid days, with Bennie curled up at my feet and Christy or Sam on my lap, sometimes both of them.

When spring finally broke and the flowers started up, Bennie and I began to take our walks again. It was easy—no pain or trouble breathing. By late April I was walking two to three miles with Bennie. He'd get tired, but not me.

We got along good through all the next year until Christy died in June 1992. She just ran out of life. Losing her was a shock because she'd been with me for so long. I missed her so much through the rest of that summer that I felt like crying whenever I thought of her. Then in September a big ol' stray whom I called Stinker showed up and helped me feel better. He'd caught a mouse and wanted to stay. There's no way I could've turned him out. Though at the time I wondered how I'd feed him, but somehow we've managed.

In the five years since my surgery, I've become more religious. I have a greater sense of being near God now. People wonder how "that old lady" gets along living alone with her animals. I'm not alone. Absolutely not alone. God is with me all the time. I'm not afraid of death, either, because I know I'll be going to a better place when He calls me. Anytime God wants to take me home, I'm ready to go. I just think of how wonderful it's going to be. There will be no suffering and no pain. We'll all be happy. I still have the St. Francis prayer that Dr. Sauvage gave me. I use it as a book marker in my Bible and read it every day.

I've had another operation since my heart surgery. Dr. Beck

found a lump in my right breast three years ago. It was cancer! After what I'd been through with my heart, that operation wasn't much, and I did fine. The trouble is those cancer pills I have to take. They cost so much.

Last week, my neighbor Pat and I were talking about what makes life worthwhile for me. I told her, "It's doing things for others and being thankful for what I have." I get down on my knees every night and thank God for another day of life. And if I've done something to help somebody that day, I'm glad. All I can give is a smile, a cheery "hello," and lend a hand because I don't have anything else. But I'm glad I can at least do that.

Forgiving another person isn't easy for any of us, but we must all learn to do this. Forgiving my dad was very difficult for me. When I was growing up he told me many times that he hated me, and I can still feel the hurt to this day. Daddy died when he was 85, and I took care of him in the last weeks of his life. Just before he died he called to me, and I sat down by his bed and, while holding his hand, said, "What do you want, Daddy?" He said in a weak voice, almost a whisper, "I've got to ask you something. Will you forgive me for the way I treated you?" I said, "I forgave you a long time ago." When I said that he became peaceful and squeezed my hand as best he could, and a short time later, he died. I didn't tell him how long it had taken me to forgive him or how hard it had been for me to do so. Yet when I had been finally able to do that, I, too, had felt God's presence and peace.

My pets are like my children at this time of my life. You bet—we have some great conversations! I've had Bennie since he was a pup. I've had Sam for a long time, too, and Stinker's been part of the family now for three-and-a-half years. Life would be empty for me without them. You know, there are a lot of apartments where they won't let you have pets. That's why I'd never leave here. What would happen to them if I moved? And to me?

I live in the present. Sure, I think about the past and enjoy it, but I don't overdo it. I also think about the future, but the present is where I am. When I wake up in the morning, I'm raring to go. I got up this morning at 4:30 because I wanted to get things done around the house. I like to get my work done early and then take a walk with Bennie. At 8:30, after I'd finished the housework, we took off and walked three miles. That ain't bad for an old lady with two artificial valves and two bypass grafts in her heart, who has had cancer, too.

Comments by Dr. Sauvage

I remember Julia's operation vividly because I encountered so much calcium in the big artery that carried blood from her heart to her body, that I doubted I could get her out of the operating room alive. I became frightened when I tried to cut into this vessel to expose the severely diseased main outlet valve of her heart because its wall had become like bone. At that point, I had no alternative but to go ahead, for I knew that Julia would surely die if we backed out without improving the function of her heart. Because of this fact, I took heavy scissors and scrunched through the rigid wall. I feared that I couldn't close this opening and she would bleed to death in the surgery. But somehow after replacing her diseased valves and grafting her blocked coronary arteries, I got it closed and she survived to regain her spunk and go home to take care of her pets, who are "family" to her.

We all need someone to love, and we need to be loved in return. It's a fact that many elderly people who live alone but have a pet do better and live longer than those who do not. It's an important concept that a furry, or even a feathered, companion can enhance the emotional life and therefore the physical health of an elderly person who would otherwise be forced to live in isolation. Imagine the surprise of a pet-store owner if he or she were to receive a prescription from Dr. Smith for his widowed patient, Mrs. Jones, age 75, who lives alone, for "One spayed, friendly cat, preferably declawed." This cat could give Mrs. Jones something to live for and be more effective and less expensive than medications to treat her depression.

Julia continues to do well despite having had to undergo cancer surgery and chemotherapy since her heart surgery. I believe that her indomitable spirit proclaiming thanks to the Lord enables her to be happy from early morning to late at night, as she accepts what comes and takes care of Bennie, Sam and Stinker. There are millions of people with far more material goods than Julia who do not have the happiness she does. Her message to them and to all of us is as clear and as simple as her life—"God is my Boss!"

Life Is a Gift
Worth Fighting For

Marta Fike Boyle

My early life is a blur, and that's probably just as well, from what they tell me. I was born 33 years ago with a seriously malformed heart that allowed very little blood to reach my lungs; a throat and stomach that were not connected (there was a wide separation, a gap, between the upper and lower portions of my esophagus), thus making it impossible for me to swallow; only one kidney that worked; and a uterus that could never function. It's a miracle that I didn't die during infancy from any one of many near-death experiences or during my strange and almost equally dangerous childhood. What I can tell you about those periods of my life is based on stories that Mom and Dad and other relatives have told me.

Dr. Sauvage operated to correct my swallowing problem when I was eight hours old. Because the upper and lower portions of my esophagus were very far apart, he had to free both segments extensively and then stretch them tightly to make their ends meet so he could stitch them together. As a result of this marked tension, the area where they were joined became a hard scar, with only a tiny opening, too small even for fluid to pass. Because of this blockage, when the saliva from my mouth had filled my throat, it would spill over into my windpipe, and cause me to choke and turn a darker shade of blue.

When Dr. Sauvage repaired my esophagus, he knew I would have this problem. So after closing my chest, he opened my abdomen and made a small opening in my stomach through which he placed one end of a special tube. After stitching this end in place, he brought the other end out through a small opening in my left side just below my ribs. This tube provided a direct channel into my stomach through which I would be fed for two and a half years.

I spent the first three months of my life in the intensive care unit of Children's Hospital in Seattle, where I was often expected to die. After that critical early period, the doctors decided to see if I could make it at home. They knew Mom had a cool head and that during my months in the hospital she had learned to do most everything that the nurses did for me. It must have been quite an emotional sight when Mom headed home with a ton of supplies and tiny me, still teetering on the edge of life.

In preparation for my homecoming, Mom and Dad had turned their bedroom into a personal intensive care unit for me. They had even installed the same type of suction machine that the nurses used in the hospital to remove the saliva and mucous from my throat when I would start to choke. After I was home,

Mom and Dad got very good at using this machine and even better at knowing from the gurgling sound of my breathing that I was filling up and needed to be suctioned immediately. Because Dad had to work, the major burden of caring for me fell on Mom. She could never get out of earshot or doze off for long because my crises were so frequent, day and night.

For many months, I made a gurgling racket with every breath I took due to the saliva that was always in my throat. When that fluid would overflow into my lungs, I couldn't get enough air, and this sense of suffocation would make me struggle harder to try and get more breath. This crisis happened many times during the day and night, and Mom or Dad would have to suction my throat immediately. Since these drowning episodes happened so often in my early life, my folks kept my little bed right next to theirs during my first year so they could respond to my critical needs as rapidly as possible.

Before they'd even try to catch a little sleep, they'd first look and listen to see if I was worse than "normal" before they'd dare doze off. It's a wonder that either of them ever got any sleep and, when they did, that I was still alive when they awoke. It's a good thing that Mom was a light sleeper because I had another problem during my early months. My heart would frequently stop, too! When that happened, I would gasp for breath, and the added noise would wake her up so she could take action to get my circulation going before my brain would be damaged by lack of oxygen. These episodes got to be known as "another of Marta's spells." It seems that while I couldn't make up my mind to live, I refused to die. Usually I came back quickly, but following one such spell a few weeks after I had been sent home, my heart appeared to stop for good. Mom tells it this way:

I was rocking Marta, who weighed only six pounds, when she quietly and with no warning stopped breathing and soon appeared pale and lifeless. I was already well-versed in what to do and quickly began to compress the chest wall over her heart in a rhythmic manner to circulate the blood. After every fourth compression I breathed into her tiny mouth to inflate her lungs so the blood flowing through them would be enriched by oxygen. After doing these resuscitative measures for a couple minutes, she took a few breaths on her own and began to get color back. Then she stopped again and once more became limp, pale and unresponsive. I immediately began to resuscitate her again, and within a few minutes she was breathing and moving once more. But by then I knew that this was not just another of her spells. It was far more serious. I feared that if her heart was to stop again, I would be unable to restart it. I realized that I had to get help, reached for the phone, and called our local ambulance to come quickly. Then after another terrifying episode of her heart suddenly stopping and then slowly starting up, I called Blackie Joslin, Marta's pediatrician, who had become like a member of the family. He said to take her to the emergency room of our nearby community hospital where he would meet us. After saying that he ran out of an office full of patients, jumped in his car and raced to get there before us.

After what seemed like forever, the ambulance screeched to a halt in front of our house. I ran out with Marta in my arms and got in, leaving my other three children, who were small and very much afraid, with a total stranger, a new neighbor who had just happened in to register to vote because I was the town clerk. As we sped to the hospital, Marta's heart stopped once more. When we pulled into the emergency driveway with a rush, I jumped out and ran in with Marta, who was breathing again. Dr. Joslin was waiting for us. He checked her over, and during the next 20 minutes she improved so much he thought that he could drive us in his car to Children's Hospital, which was 12 miles away. He wanted Dr. Sauvage to see Marta there. So off we went. But Marta's heart hadn't stabilized! It stopped several more times on the way to the hospital, and each time I became her heart and lungs, while Dr. Joslin weaved through the heavy traffic as fast as he could go. It seemed like we would never get there.

Many years later, they told me the worst part of that trip was when we got stuck in a traffic jam for 15 minutes while the crowd left the University of Washington stadium after a football game. I can just imagine the panic that Mother and Dr. Joslin must have felt during that ride to Children's. When they finally got to the hospital, Dr. Joslin leaped out of the car and ran in with me cradled in his arms. To everyone's amazement, after I was in the intensive care unit, my heart stabilized. A few days later Dr. Joslin and Dr. Sauvage sent me home again to try and survive.

Before I went home the first time, Dr. Sauvage had passed small catheters down my throat on two occasions to stretch the scar tissue that blocked my swallowing. Because I got much worse both times he did this, Dr. Sauvage decided to leave my esophagus alone and see what nature could do for it. To everyone's delight, after about a year I could swallow my saliva and didn't have to be suctioned day and night. Then Dr. Sauvage began an extended program in which he gently stretched my esophagus once a week at the Children's Hospital over a period of several months. My swallowing improved little by little, until I could finally take a bottle without choking.

Though my progress was slow, by the time I was two-and-a-half years old I ate well enough that Mom and Dad didn't have to feed me through the tube anymore, which was a big relief for them because they could stop worrying that I might accidentally pull it out. In my earlier days I did that many times, and each time, one or both of them would have to rush me to Children's Hospital to have a new one inserted before the opening could close off.

During my first year Mom was with me constantly because other people were afraid I would die on them. Then her mother began to provide a few hours of relief. Thank heavens for Grandma, or Mom wouldn't have made it either.

My development was slow. I didn't turn over for the first year. I just lay there trying to breathe and stay alive. I never crawled and didn't begin to walk until I was four. I didn't say anything until I was three, and I couldn't speak intelligibly for nine more years. There were so many sounds I couldn't make that even Mom had trouble understanding me. If you think that all of this was hard on me, just think of my parents. And it was no picnic for my two brothers and my sister because my parents had to focus so much of their attention on me.

Because of the way my heart was formed, not enough blood could get to my lungs. This caused me to be short of oxygen and gave my skin a bluish hue. When I attempted to do even little things, I'd turn deep blue, become short of breath, and tire quickly. For my first few years, Dr. Sauvage felt that open-heart surgery to correct the defects inside my heart would be too dangerous because of my small size and frail condition. Instead, when I was five years old, he placed an artificial graft between the artery going to my left arm and the artery going to my left lung, so that more blood could get to my lungs. That surgery really helped, but three years later the graft collapsed, and then I was worse than ever. After that setback I became blue again and was so weak and short of breath that I had to be carried from place to place. About all I could do on my own was sit.

Now there was no choice. Even *I* knew that it was either get my heart fixed or die. But Mom and Dad told me very little about what Dr. Sauvage was going to do. There was a part of me that understood that reasoning—you don't want to overwhelm the kid—but there was a part of me that wanted to know more. Fear was the main focus of my life at that point. The time waiting for my open-heart surgery was a scary, helpless experience, made worse each time I'd turn real blue because then someone would place an oxygen mask over my face and make me feel like I was suffocating. I was too weak to fight them off.

During the weeks before my operation, I spent all my time on the couch in the family room. When I had to go to the bathroom, Mom or Dad carried me. At night Dad would carry me to my bed, tuck me in and stay with me until I fell asleep. During those weeks he began a pattern of doing affirmations while I drifted off. He'd place one hand on my forehead and the other over my heart and say these affirmations each night. The ones I remember are: "God will soon be fixing your heart, and Dr. Sauvage is going to help. You will become strong like your friends. You will heal very quickly. You will have no bleeding or pain. Your heart will work perfectly. This is a time of great joy because you are about to start a wonderful new life." Pretty powerful messages to give the subconscious. To this day I believe that this form of prayer had a big impact in making my surgery a marvelous success.

This communication between Dad and me enabled my mind to shift from fear to faith and determination. It was one of the most emotionally and spiritually empowering experiences that I've ever had. I remember sitting up in bed the night before my open-heart surgery and thinking, "I've got too much to do to let this be the end. I'm only eight years old."

The next morning Dr. Sauvage repaired the inside of my mixed-up heart so it could function normally. Mom and Dad told me that he stayed with me all night after my operation to make sure I was okay. Everything went well, and I went home nine days later with a pink complexion.

I've had no further problems with my heart. But I still have a little trouble swallowing. I have to be careful, even now, about what I eat and remember to chew my food thoroughly. When swallowing gets too difficult—every year or two—I have my throat stretched again.

I don't remember much of my early years because I've blocked out a lot. But of the memories I do have, school was the worst. My garbled speech was a big problem not only in class, but outside as well. The early years were especially bad. My classmates teased me without letup day after day about how I spoke, about being little, about not being able to keep up with them, about not being able to eat like they did, and about choking whenever I tried to do so.

My first five grades in school were an endless, bitter experience. After I'd get home my family would boost me back up emotionally, but the next day when I'd go back to school my tormentors would crush me down again. My only defense was to keep quiet. I wouldn't say anything because I was terrified of everyone, and I knew that they couldn't understand me anyway. Apprehension made my swallowing worse, and if I took a drink of water at school it would go down my windpipe and make me choke. I wanted to get away, to sneak out when no one was looking, and go home where I would be safe. Yet there was something in me that refused to give up. I was determined to live. I had come too far to turn back.

Mom knew that my speech problems had to be overcome if I were ever to live a normal life. She got top professional help and started me on intensive speech therapy when I was five and continued my lessons until I was 13 and in the seventh grade. Fortunately, my speech started to improve significantly when I was in the sixth grade. In fact, by the end of that year I spoke well enough that most of the kids stopped teasing me. I continued my lessons for another year and improved still more. By the time I was in high school, I could speak as well as anyone, and this helped me develop confidence in myself. As this happened, my classmates began to accept me. Having them do that was a wondrously fulfilling experience after having been an outsider for so long.

During my high school days I thought a lot about who I was, where I was going, and why God had kept me alive. I grew up rapidly during that period of my life and came to believe I had survived for a reason. In my own way, I believe I'm here to teach. There are some people I can help because of what I've been through that others might not be able to reach. The main lesson I have to teach is the great value of life. We must never take this gift for granted, and we must never give up. If my parents and doctors had given up on me, or if I had given up on myself, I would have been dead long ago.

Though I was no academic star in school, I never failed a grade despite all my physical problems. Learning didn't come easy for me, but I made up by hard work what I lacked in ability. I did my best, and I'm proud of my C average.

I graduated from high school just after turning 19, which isn't bad, considering I was only able to go to school for three months during the second grade, the year I had my open-heart surgery. It would have been better if I had been held back a year because from that time on I was always playing catch-up.

After graduating from high school, I started working with children. Since I had missed out on so much in my weird childhood, I really enjoyed playing with the children I took care of. I did a lot of that, a lot of getting into the "little girl within me," just playing, which I couldn't do as a sickly child.

After doing child care for several years, I decided to do something I had wanted to do for a long time. I became an apprentice plumber and worked at my trade in new construction for three years, until my back forced me to give it up. When that happened, I was only six months away from becoming a licensed plumber, a goal I so wanted to achieve. But during the time I was able to work, I just had a ball and loved every day of it. My job was to set and install toilets, sinks, dishwashers and water heaters. I could outwork a lot of the men, and because I'm only 4 feet 11 inches, I could easily get into spaces that were too small for many of them. I was proud to be a good plumber and wish I could still be doing it. Now I do housecleaning, and I'm happy that I can do this work. It's easier on my back.

Cal and I met at a motivational seminar when I was a senior. We were attracted to each other from the start, but we didn't begin to get serious for about a year. Marriage is a commitment for a lifetime; it's not something to jump in and out of. My folks are a perfect example of this. When I came into their lives everything changed for them, but they didn't panic. They did what they had to do and they have had a happy life, both because of and in spite of me. If I could've picked my parents, I would've chosen the ones I have, because no other parents could've given me so much loving care.

After a year of casual dating, Cal and I began to realize that something special was developing between us. After a few more months, we knew we were made for each other, and three years after our first meeting we were married. Though that special day seems like it was yesterday, it's hard to believe that it was really ten years ago. And while time has passed so fast for us, the best thing is that our love has continued to grow.

We struggled financially for the first few years, but we were happy anyway. Our finances are better now. Cal is a talented restaurant kitchen designer and equipment supplier. He had few clients at first, but with persistence and more experience he has developed a fine reputation in his specialized field and is now doing well.

Finding happiness is what life is all about. I find my happiness by being with people I care about and from helping those who need me. I can never get enough sharing time with friends, who mean a lot to me. I try to create quality, one-on-one time to be with my girlfriends, especially those who have been in my life for a long time. This is harder now that we're all married and doing our own thing. I gain happiness from taking care of Grandma, who has Alzheimer's disease. She was there when I needed her, and it's my turn now to be there for her.

I believe that good can come from adversity. Take me, for example. There are spiritual positives that have come as a result of all the operations and trials I've been through. For one thing, our family grew closer because of the challenging times we went through together. And I have gained a different perspective of life than had I been born normal. I doubt there are many people who value life as much as I do. When you've had to fight for your life one day at a time over many years, you look at it as a gift from God, not as a right.

I would never take senseless risks, like bungee-jumping. Life is too precious, and it could be gone in an instant. My experiences have taught me a lot about the importance of people, of family time, of friends, of being supported emotionally, and of honest, free communication. Nothing is as important as another person. Life together is all we have, and if we can't take time to value and pay tribute to that, then what is there? Happiness doesn't come from things; it comes from people and doing for others.

People who are hurting don't want to listen to what I've been through. They want me to listen to them and help with their problems. I find that I can always be of some assistance to those who need me if I'm open to them. I know I can't change the world or a lot of people, but I can help a few and that's good enough for me. I know my limits, and I'm satisfied with who I am.

Because Cal and I know that we can never have children of our own, we're planning to adopt a baby. To get ready for that day I've started doing volunteer work at the Children's Hospital, and I love it.

Comments by Dr. Sauvage

Marta's problems were different from those of the other patients in this book. Her problems were congenital, meaning that she was born with them, while the other nine patients developed their problems after they were born. Problems that develop after birth are called acquired. Only about one percent of heart disease is congenital and Marta's type of "blue baby" disease, which medically is called the Tetralogy of Fallot, accounts for only a tiny fraction of that small figure. The combination of Marta's heart condition with her other problems is as rare as getting hit by lightning twice during the same storm and living to tell about it.

The amazing thing is not that an occasional baby is born with an abnormality, but rather that so many babies are born totally normal. Consider for a moment that each of us was formed from two cells (sperm and ovum) that united to form a single cell, which divided to become two new cells, and those two divided to become four, and those four became eight, and so on until eventually, in some completely mysterious manner, we became the 100,000,000,000,000 cells that form the 11 major organ systems that comprise the physical you and me. I am constantly amazed by the grandeur and majesty of the human body, let alone the soul.

Marta and her parents are very special to me because of the severity of the problems she was born with, and because I've been privileged to know her and her folks now for 33 years. Perhaps because Mary Ann and I have a large family, we can, at least in part, appreciate Marta's courage and that of her parents. We can imagine what an impact Marta would've had on our lives had she been born to us.

Marta never knew anything other than the way she was in her early years. But later she came to understand that she was not like the other children. She couldn't swallow, run or play, nor even talk the way they did. As parents, Mary Ann and I can appreciate the pain and agony that her parents must have suffered as they saw their child struggle just to survive.

While there is no question that Marta's success in life is a tribute to her parents, she has put it all together, too. Marta wasted little precious time crying, "Why me?" She came to accept who she was and to appreciate herself and each day as precious gifts from God. As a result, she is today a well-adjusted, happy person.

Thank You, God, for Another Day

Patsy Paris

My life has been on the dark side many times, but through the grace of God I've survived and found happiness, especially in recent years. I've had a deep spirituality all my life. God's never been more than a hand-touch away. Even now. Every day, every hour. People don't believe that. A lot of people don't. But it's true.

I was lucky to be born into a loving family on July 9, 1935, the third of four children, in the little coal-mining community of Grangertown, Kentucky, population 150, during the poorest of times. Though we had next to nothing, I never felt unloved or unwanted by my parents. They were special people who often said "I love you" to each other and to us children. Those words and feelings were priceless gifts that held our family close.

Mom was a devout Southern Baptist who ran our home with love and order, while Dad worked in a hazardous coal mine for a meager wage. But my dad was smart, and knew he had to find another job before a mine-shaft accident could take his life. He did, and when I was two, we moved across the state line into Evansville, Indiana, where he had found a job working on the Chrysler assembly line. Though that employment had no job security, it was better than breathing coal dust in the semidarkness of a damp, cold labyrinth deep down within the earth. After two years of putting auto parts together and never knowing when the line would close down, he got a more permanent position as a switchman for the Union Pacific's railroad terminal in Evansville. Although Dad was thankful to have his new job, he really wanted to move us to California. Five years later he was lucky and obtained a better job with the Southern Pacific in Los Angeles, and shortly after that we moved to Glendale, an adjacent suburb. Dad worked there for that railroad from 1944 until he retired in 1963, progressing from switchman to brakeman, and, in his last few years, to control tower operator.

We were a happy family. Mom took care of us and Dad made enough for our needs and a bit more. Because I was nimble and had a good sense of rhythm, Mom started me taking dancing lessons when I was in the fifth grade. My teacher said I had natural talent, and by the time I finished the eighth grade, I was a good tap and acrobatic dancer.

When I started my freshman year of high school, I had just turned 15 and had never dated a boy. I wasn't ready for that. My world was simple and happy. Then all of that changed in a single moment after a back-to-school dance in early

September 1950. I shall refer to the man I will tell you about as "George," though that's not his real name. He was 25, a talented commercial artist, an accomplished pianist and the son of prominent parents who lived close by. Though he was too old to be a member of our youth group, he occasionally played the piano for us. On one such occasion, a week before the dance, he said he'd like to go if he had a date. The next day a girlfriend in the group asked me if I would go with him. Me! I had never even been to a school dance, and besides, he was ten years older than me. I was startled. Not knowing what else to say, I replied, "I'll ask Mom and Dad."

I did, and after they had thought about it they said I could go with him because his parents were fine people, and everyone else in my youth group was going too. Dad also said, "He's older and will take good care of you." But I was still apprehensive.

Saturday night arrived, and George drove up in his 1948 white Pontiac sedan. He opened the door for me and we left for the dance. On the way there he said very little, and I said nothing. The silence was frightening. When we got there, he parked in the school lot and we went in. I was uneasy from the start. Something didn't feel right, but I didn't know what it was or what to do. I wanted to go home and was glad when the last dance was finally over.

We started home, and I couldn't wait to get there. But then for no apparent reason he slowed down and turned onto a dark side road overgrown with brush. I was scared and said, "Where are we going?" He didn't answer. By then I was terrified. When we couldn't see the main road anymore, he stopped the car and turned the lights off. My heart was beating so hard it shook my chest. The moon was full, and in that eerie halflight I could sense that George was about to do something terrible to me. But before I could open the door to escape, he was on top of me, pulling my skirt up. I tried to push him away but I couldn't. I screamed and fought, but I couldn't hold him back. I was being pinned. Straight down into hell.

When it was finally over, I was in shock and couldn't stop crying. I don't remember much about going home except for George telling me that I *had* to do these things because guys expected this from girls they took out and spent money on.

This was my first date, and I was in no way, size or shape a street-smart kid. All this was a monstrous shock to me. He told me to shut up and never say anything about what he'd done. When we got home he said, "Get out, and remember what I told you."

I ran sobbing to my room, where I cried until I finally fell asleep near dawn. I felt betrayed, ashamed, violated and totally alone. I couldn't tell my parents or anyone what had happened.

I was awakened a few hours later by my entire family standing around my bed. I was terrified and thought, "Do they know?" Then Dad started laughing and said, "Young lady, I want you to get up and look in the mirror." Someone had looked in and seen my face and called the rest. When I looked in the mirror, I knew why. I had broken out with chicken pox; there wasn't a white spot on my face or neck. I was burning up with fever, but that was nothing compared with the suffering going on inside me.

While I was recovering from the chicken pox, I cried and prayed and thought, "This is a secret between God and me." I knew that if I told Mom and Dad, it would hurt them terribly. I'd never wanted to hurt anyone, let alone them. So I thought, "He's gone and it'll never happen again. I'll be okay." But it didn't turn out that way. And bingo! Guess what? Uh-huh, one-time shot.

My periods had started two years before, and they were regular. My next one was due shortly after I went back to school. It didn't come. I asked a girlfriend what this could mean and she said, in jest, "Maybe you're pregnant."

I smiled weakly and walked away in fear.

Four weeks after raping me, George, who had been drafted into the army because of the Korean War, left for Camp Carson near Colorado Springs, Colorado. I hoped I'd never see him again.

I waited and prayed for my period to start, but nothing happened, and my fears grew by the day. I wanted to hide, but there was no place to go. Then I started to vomit each morning after breakfast. Now there was no doubt in my mind. *I was pregnant.* I got George's address from his parents and wrote him what he'd done to me. There was no answer. I felt totally alone and very frightened. I thought, "What would Mom say if she knew?"

At first I could conceal my vomiting from her by leaving the breakfast table when I felt the first wave of nausea coming on, but one morning it came so fast that I couldn't get away in time and vomited all over the floor. I couldn't hide what had happened to me from her anymore and fell sobbing into her outstretched arms. She knew and said, "I love you," as she hugged me tight. When Dad came home, Mom told him what had happened and he hugged me, too. I was relieved, at least, that now they knew.

My folks stood by me in their own way, though "their way" might seem harsh today. They said, "We have to do what's right." They went to see George's parents and told them what he'd done. On hearing this they broke down and wept. But neither they nor my parents ever considered having the baby aborted. To them, a life was a life, no matter the circumstances or age. I didn't even know what the word "abortion" meant and asked Mom. I was shocked when she told me.

George's parents said that he would honor his responsibilities and marry me. My parents agreed that this would be best for the baby, and we should do it soon. I was never consulted. It's what I had to do, though even the thought of marrying him was repulsive to me.

When I was 10 weeks pregnant, George got leave and came home for the wedding. It was a somber affair during which I wouldn't let him touch me. Reverend Goodwin, pastor of our Baptist church, married us in the living room of my folks' home on November 21, 1950. He was the one person besides my parents who helped me feel I'd survive. After this bitter ceremony, George went back to the army and I went back to the ninth grade—pregnant, 15, and now married to this man of 25, whom I despised.

I had a terrible time throughout my pregnancy. I didn't stop vomiting until after the fourth month. I became water-logged and my weight increased from 99 to 157 pounds. Toward the end I looked like a balloon. After the sixth month, my blood pressure went up and my kidneys wouldn't work right. Even so, I went to school. But without Mom and Dad's and Rev. Goodwin's support, I couldn't have found the courage to face my classmates and teachers day after day while my "condition" became ever more obvious.

I finished school in late May and a few days later went into labor. My folks rushed me to the hospital and then stayed in the waiting room until my baby was born. I vividly remember the sign on the outer door of the O.B. floor: "No One Under 18 Allowed." My nurse said it didn't apply to me.

Having a baby at 15 was bewildering and scary. My contractions were very painful and went on for 40 hours. I bled a lot and nearly died. Finally, my baby was born weighing 9 pounds, 12 ounces and measuring 22 inches long. When I first saw her I knew she was a gift from God. She was beautiful. She was mine, and I named her Cindy. I never thought of her as belonging to George. Yet I was legally his wife and he was her biological father.

During my stay in the hospital, Dr. Knox, my obstetrician, and his entire staff made me feel at home, wanted and very important. These special people inspired me to want to become a nurse, and that desire changed my life. If they hadn't, I could've lost it all. If I'd been in some other hospital, who knows what would've happened to me? As it was, my ambition seemed only a distant dream, a fantasy, since I'd only finished the ninth grade and there seemed no way I could ever go further.

Cindy and I went home with Mom and Dad. They loved her, and so did George's parents. After a few weeks, my weight dropped back to 99 pounds and I felt good again. What a relief! Even though I couldn't bear to think of George, I loved Cindy with all my heart. When she began to smile, I melted inside. She was a good feeder, and it was a joy to hold her close while she nursed. I was sad when my milk dried up after nine months, but she took to the bottle and cereal just as well.

A few months after we'd been with my folks, George began sending letters demanding that Cindy and I come to Camp Carson and live with him. But just the thought of being near that man terrified me. We were happy at home with Mom and Dad, and I didn't want to leave. But this became harder and harder to avoid after he began threatening my parents with legal action unless I complied with his order.

Finally, we had to go. With tear-filled eyes and so choked up that I couldn't speak, I kissed Mom and Dad goodbye and climbed aboard the Southern Pacific passenger train to head east with Cindy and all we had. I remember the terror of that moment when the train pulled out of the station taking my baby, who was but ten months, and me, 16 years old, to join her father, the man who had raped me. The trip to Colorado Springs with its several connections was long and fearful, and I had to sit up the entire time. I was shaking like a leaf when we finally arrived, for I knew there was now no choice—I had to get off and confront him. As I came down the steps holding Cindy with one arm and our belongings with the other, I caught sight of George and wanted to turn and run. But he had seen me, too, and there was no escape. He came forward to meet us, and to my utter surprise, he was actually pleasant.

George took us to his car, and we headed for the base and our new home. Though it was scary being with him, he was civil to me for the first few days. Then the real George, the man who had attacked me, began to come out. Soon, I found to my horror that he was even worse than I had feared. He was a drunkard, a compulsive gambler, and a womanizer of the crudest sort. He had escapades with one pickup after another. He even brought some of those loose women into our quarters and flaunted them in front of me. But as far as I was concerned, they could have him. I wanted no part of him; I just wanted to be left alone.

In addition to his lecherous nature, George was physically abusive to me, gave me little money, and wouldn't let me drive "his" car. I was to stay "home," if you could call it that. When his women would keep him away for several nights at a time, I was thankful. I never felt safe when he was with us, and I prayed that he would disappear and never return.

After George was discharged from the army in 1953, we returned to Glendale. My life with him at Camp Carson had

been a degrading experience that I still find hard to think
about, even now. His outside women were never enough to
satisfy him. He had to have me, too. George was an animal
when it came to sex, and I couldn't stop him. Despite all I
could do, he still got me pregnant three times in the next four
years, before I had to have an emergency hysterectomy
because of profuse uterine hemorrhage. Though the children—Norm born in 1954, Sandy in 56 and Terry in 57—were
not conceived in love, they were nonetheless precious gifts
from God to me. Each was special and unique, a creation for
eternity. I couldn't have survived without them, nor could I
have survived without my Creator being near. It was hard,
and I spent many nights after the children were asleep just
lying on the bed, crying, until the early morning hours. I
prayed to God that what had happened to me would never
happen to them.

Though George was a talented commercial artist and made
plenty of money, I had to beg for what little I got. I was scared
to be near him and I never knew when he'd strike me. He beat
me the most severely of all when I was six months pregnant
with Sandy. It's a wonder I didn't lose her. Because he was
getting worse and worse, I knew I had to prepare to support
myself and the children so that one day we could escape from
him. But how? I'd only finished the ninth grade and had four
small children to raise. Before I could do anything, I knew I
first had to finish high school or obtain an equivalency certificate. There was no way I could go to high school for three
years, but the certification alternative seemed feasible, since
I'd been studying and reading at home ever since I'd gone to
live with George at Camp Carson in 1952. Before I could take
the examination, though, I had to attend a six-week night
course from 7:00 to 10:00 each Monday, Wednesday and Friday.

I made arrangements to take that course in the spring of 1957 and then told George what I was going to do. As expected, he went into a violent rage. I thought he was going to beat me, but instead he stormed out of the house to get drunk, cursing as he slammed the door behind him. I was relieved. This was better than I'd anticipated.

I went to the classes, and George didn't try to stop me. My sister, Dee, and a neighbor girlfriend took turns looking after the children. I got an 83 on the comprehensive examination at the end of the course and received my certificate in late June. I was very proud because this certificate was essential if the children and I were ever to have a chance of escaping from George's abuse.

I now took the step I'd longed to take since I gave birth to Cindy. This was my time to reach for the sky. I applied to the Glendale Adventist Hospital to become a licensed practical nurse and was ecstatic when they accepted me. The hospital made a special curriculum just for me, in which I'd be trained by three wonderful nurses with whom I'd work eight hours a day, five days a week, for a little over two years. I started this exciting period of my life in the fall of 1957, after I stopped breast-feeding Terry. Dee and my girlfriend continued to take care of the children while I was at the hospital, even though I couldn't pay them.

On an April night in 1959, my relations with George reached their lowest point. He arrived home drunk, as expected, but was even more belligerent than usual. When he began shouting, I was seized with fear, and Sandy, who was barely three, started to cry. In a frenzy he grabbed her and screamed, "Shut up!" as he threw her against the wall with all his force. She fell to the floor and lay there, limp. I thought he had killed her! For an instant I froze and couldn't believe what had happened. Then I rushed across the room and picked her up. Though stunned, she turned her head and started to cry a little. I cradled her in my arms, ran to the phone and called the police before he could stop me. Fortunately, there was a squad car in the neighborhood and two officers came to the door within minutes. George resisted arrest, but they quickly took him away despite his cursing and efforts to escape. In the morning I got a restraining order that forbade him from entering the house or in any way interfering with the children and me. I still thank God that Sandy wasn't seriously injured.

While the restraining order was a blessing, it didn't keep George, who was only held in jail for a few days, from subsequently trying to break in. He'd try to do this at least once a month, generally between 3:00 and 4:00 in the morning after the bars had closed. On those occasions the children and I would be awakened by his incessant pounding on the front door and by the obscenities he screamed at us as he tried to batter his way in. We lived in mortal fear that he would succeed.

In spite of all this, I did well in my nurse's training and enjoyed every minute of it. I loved nursing because it combined the joys of helping sick people with the excitement of learning. I was the proudest person in the world when I got my diploma in January 1960 because for me to have become a practical nurse was equivalent to someone else becoming a medical doctor. My diploma made me feel that nothing could stop me. I'd defeated this man who had abused me and told me over and over that I was worthless and could never do anything. All lies! I had gone for the gold and won.

Now I could get a job and take care of the children. I had been paid $.75 an hour during my first year of training and $1.00 during my second year. Now I could make three times that amount.

I had planned to work at the Adventist Hospital in Glendale, where they'd been so good to me, but two nights after graduating I came to realize how dangerous it would be for us to remain there. George, in another drunken frenzy, stormed the house at about 3:00 A.M. He pounded and kicked the door with such force that I thought for sure it would soon give way. The walls shook so violently that pictures fell to the floor. I feared for our lives and called the police. Four patrol units came quickly, and after a brief struggle the officers took him away. To our dismay they released him the next day. By then the children and I were too frightened to stay in Glendale any longer because of what he might do to us. I called my parents in San Bernardino, where they lived at that time, 60 miles away, and told them we were moving there as soon as we could. They were delighted and said, "It's about time!"

The next day my cousin, Jim Fowler, drove over to see me. He parked a 1956 Ford Galaxy in front of the house, came in, gave me the keys and said, "It's yours!" You can imagine my surprise, total delight and gratitude. That car, along with my diploma, meant I could be independent, drive to San Bernardino, and establish a safe home for the children and me.

Somehow George had learned about my car, and during the night he got his revenge by slashing all the tires. In the morning when we looked out and saw what he had done, we were devastated. But when Dad and Dee's husband arrived later in the morning with a rented truck to move us, I knew we could escape. By midafternoon they had replaced the tires and packed us up. The children and I said a prayer of thanks as we drove off because Glendale had been a place of uncertainty, fear and siege for us. My parents welcomed us with open arms when we arrived, and though crowded, we stayed with them for a week while I located an apartment nearby. Then we moved into our new home to begin our life afresh, full of joyous anticipation.

Soon there was an opening on the nursing staff of St. Bernardine's Hospital, paying $2.75 an hour. They accepted me and I gladly went to work the next morning; bills had to be paid. Mom and Dad took care of the children after school until I could get home from the hospital.

A few weeks later, I filed for divorce and asked for full custody of the children. This was quickly granted and finalized in September of 1960. At last we were free. George was ordered to pay $75 monthly for the support of each child. He paid nothing the first year, claiming he had no money. The court asked for his tax returns, but rather than surrender them he started to pay up. Even so, his child-support payments were always erratic and never complete. Somehow, though, the children and I got along. We made up for our lack of material goods by what was in our hearts.

Although I enjoyed working at St. Bernardine's, my goal was to be appointed to the nursing staff of the Loma Linda University Teaching Hospital, which was 12 miles away. When that opportunity came in 1962, I took it and worked there until June of 1971. The intensity of patient care at Loma Linda was a challenge that I enjoyed. I attended as many of the continuing education lectures for the nursing staff as I could in order to advance my knowledge and keep up with the times. A special feature of our work environment that was priceless to me was the prayer we said together before report in which we asked God to help us take care of our patients.

There were, however, two very sad occurrences during our life in San Bernardino. The first happened in 1964, when my dad died within minutes following a massive heart attack that occurred just after we'd finished Christmas dinner. He'd

retired a year and a half before and was enjoying those pleasant days of his life with Mom. They'd been very close, and his
passing was very difficult for her and for all of us.

The next year, John, my older brother, a 20-year career
Marine dedicated to his country and the corps, died suddenly,
also of a massive heart attack. We grieved even more when
we learned that he'd been having heart pains for several
months but hadn't sought medical attention. He thought
they'd go away. Had he received proper care, it's likely he
would've survived and been enjoying life today.

Then something very exciting happened to me in early
March of 1971. I met Gene at a dinner party, a man whom I
would soon grow to love. He was a pleasant, retiring, gracious, caring person, three years older than me. Gene was so
different from George that I was attracted to him on that
basis alone.

Gene had grown up in Belding, a farming community of
7,000 in central Michigan. When he was 17, he enlisted in the
navy during the Korean War and decided later to make it a
career. Eventually he rose to the rank of chief petty officer in
telecommunications. Gene planned to return to Belding following his scheduled retirement in July, just four months
away. We began dating, and before long it was serious. The
children liked him and he liked them. All this seemed too
good to be true. When he proposed, I accepted, and we were
married in June. Following our honeymoon in Las Vegas and
Gene's discharge after we returned, we left for Michigan,
excited by the prospects of all that lay before us.

We purchased a comfortable house in Belding and settled
down to a pleasant life in this quiet Midwestern town that was
so different from Los Angeles, with its crowded freeways and
endless people. The children entered school and made new

friends quickly. I worked the swing shift at the community hospital, which had 35 beds, and Gene delivered mail for the post office. We had a good life, and I thought we'd spend the rest of our days there.

I remember the very moment it happened, on a cold, windy, gray October afternoon in 1974. Because of low census at the hospital, after an hour my supervisor said I could go home. This was welcome news, as I had much work to get caught up on there. I came in through the back door and went upstairs to put my coat away. Gene, who'd heard me come in, met me at the door of our bedroom dressed in my clothes and wearing a pair of high-heeled women's shoes that were much too big to be mine. I was startled, but thought he might be preparing for a Halloween skit or something. Even so, I was puzzled because he was shaking and seemed very frightened. Then he said in a quivering voice, "Don't come in, someone's here."

I quickly moved to the side and could see—that "someone" was a partially disrobed man! I was stunned. My mind went blank. I had no thoughts and, at that moment, hardly any feelings. I turned, went down the stairs, and walked slowly into the kitchen, as if in a trance. I sat down at the table and just stared out the window, seeing nothing. I was in mental shock because until a few minutes before, I had not the slightest suspicion that my husband of three years was bisexual. I felt betrayed, empty, alone and abandoned. Yet in so many ways, Gene was a good person who'd always been kind and generous to the children and me. I asked God, "After the agony of George, why did this have to happen to us?"

A few minutes later, Gene's partner, now clothed, slunk down the stairs and fled through the front door. Sometime later Gene, then in his own clothes and shoes, walked furtively into the kitchen, looking at the floor.

Though it was difficult, after a few painful moments of just looking away from him, I looked up and said, "How could you do this to me?"

He said, "I didn't want to, but I can't help myself. My sexuality has been a problem for me all of my life."

"For God's sake, why did you marry me and have it come to this?" I asked.

"I thought I had a reason to give it up when I met you, but I've found I can't."

What could I do? Terry, my youngest, by now a senior in high school and my last one still at home, fortunately was not there at that moment. I wanted to keep this from her until she left home. She planned to move out after graduation, and I hoped that Gene would be willing to continue the facade of our marriage until then. He said that he'd do whatever I wanted.

"Good, you live on your side of the house, and I'll live on mine."

He replied, "I'm sorry; I understand."

The next few months weren't easy. To say the least, our relations were strained and distant. Gene and I largely ignored each other, like boarders in a rooming house. He went his way and I went mine. Nonetheless, I thanked God for what I still had—my children, my health and my job.

Terry noticed that things were different between Gene and me, but she never asked why. After graduation she obtained a job as a waitress in Belding's best restaurant and moved into an apartment with a girlfriend from school. But she still found time to stop in and see me nearly every day.

By the time my 40th birthday rolled around in July, I'd stopped feeling sorry for myself, was making the best that I could of my life, and planned to divorce Gene in the fall. Then suddenly, at 2:00 P.M. on August 26, 1975, I had my first encounter with heart disease while I was taking a shower before going to work. Without warning, I was seized by crushing pain in the middle of my chest. I could hardly breathe, and became so weak that I could barely stand. I feared I was having a heart attack and called for Gene because I had no choice. He ran into the bathroom, helped me into my robe, assisted me to the car and drove rapidly to our local hospital. After the staff in the emergency room checked me over, they said I was threatening to have a major heart attack and had to be transferred immediately by ambulance to the Blodgett Hospital in Grand Rapids.

The pain started to ease when we were about halfway there, but it came back whenever I tried to move. Dr. Raymond Fuller, who would be my cardiologist for the next eight years, was waiting for me in the emergency room as we pulled up. He said, "Hi! I'm Dr. Fuller; we'll take good care of you."

I liked him right then. He sent me directly to the coronary unit, where he directed my care. By the next morning I had, in their terms, "cooled off." The treatment had averted a major heart attack, but such a catastrophic event could still happen at any moment. Dr. Fuller made arrangements to take me to the heart catheterization laboratory to perform special X rays of the arteries (coronaries) that supplied my heart. He said he needed a road map of these supply lines to know what should be done. He explained what I already knew—that heart attacks occur when not enough blood can get through the obstructed coronary arteries to nourish the heart muscle and keep it alive. Heart pain, or angina, is nature's way of warning us when the blood supply to the heart muscle gets dangerously low. I signed the consent form.

Shortly after performing these X rays, Dr. Fuller came to see me. "Patsy, the arteries of your heart are very bad. They're either blocked or narrowed, and you need an operation to bring in new supply lines. This must be done soon."

The thought of having an operation was hard for me to accept, and after Dr. Fuller left I cried for the next three-and-a-half hours. The nurses tried to comfort me, but they knew I had to go through this period of adjustment. I thought over and over about how my dad and brother had both died from massive heart attacks. As I pondered and wept, I slowly began to appreciate that I had a chance to do something about this threat to my life that they hadn't had. After my tears stopped, I ate a little dinner and began to feel better.

That evening Dr. James Delavan, a young heart surgeon with an excellent reputation, visited me. He said, "Dr. Fuller asked me to see you because you need coronary bypass surgery."

Right then, I knew this was for real; I had to go ahead, before it was too late. Dr. Delavan was only trying to help me. He had plenty to do besides opening my chest. Terry came and I told her, and then I called Dee in California and told her, too.

The next morning, Dr. Delavan took veins from my right leg and made four grafts, which he implanted to carry blood from the big artery leaving my heart to the open downstream portions of my blocked coronary arteries. I had no problems and went home in ten days, where Gene looked after me until I could take care of myself.

With my heart now nourished by its new blood supply, I regained my strength and returned to work three months later. For the first few weeks I was okay, but then I started to get progressively weaker and more and more short of breath. As this was happening, the pain in my chest returned. I could then barely go from one unit to another in our small hospital and had to stop working. Over the next few weeks, the angina came on quicker with less exertion, lasted longer, and hurt more. Dr. Fuller gave me more medications, but they did little good. I became fatalistic and felt that if God wanted me, it was okay. The children were raised and on their own. I became depressed and thought, "I'm going to die." I didn't lose my faith, but I lost control of it. I asked time and again, "Why is this happening to me?"

Dr. Fuller was very concerned and told me that he had to do more angios to learn what should be done. Though this frightened me, I didn't want him to give up on me, so I said, "Yes." After the procedure he told me that two of my four grafts were closed, one was nearly closed, and only one was still satisfactory. Then without mincing words, he said, "This is really serious. I'll ask Dr. Delavan to see you." I was taken aback, though not really surprised. A few hours later, Dr. Delavan came to my room and said, "Patsy, we have to redo it."

I'd expected this, too. I didn't hold it against him that the operation had failed. In fact, I'd developed a high respect for him. I knew he cared and would do his best for me. Furthermore, his strong presence and confident attitude helped restore my courage and will to live. I asked, "Where are you going to get the veins?"

"We'll get them from your left leg. Don't worry about that."

"What is your survival rate in redo operations?"

"Patsy, I wouldn't take you in there if I didn't think you had a good chance. I know that with the help of the Guy upstairs, we'll get through it okay."

Bolstered by this support, I said, "Let's do it."

Dr. Delavan did my second open-heart operation in early October of 1976, just 13 months after my first. He took the veins from my left leg and used them to replace the two grafts that were closed and the one that was narrowed, and my heart again responded favorably. I went home in eight days, thanking

God I'd survived and praying that this operation wouldn't fail like my first one. As before, Gene was there to help me.

This time I waited five months before going back to work because I wanted to be sure I was all right. When I went back, I was full of energy and could race between our three units. My heart was strong and I had no pain.

I did well for the next two years and began to believe that I would have no further trouble with my heart. Midway through that period, Terry moved back to Glendale in 1977 to study commercial art. While I was glad to see her do this, I was now alone with Gene, a man who had become foreign to me, and yet he was a person to whom I owed much for the care he had given me. Though we continued to live in the same house during that period, Gene and I went our separate ways and let the question of our divorce remain unsettled.

Then the chest pains started again, little by little, but soon unmistakable. After checking me over, Dr. Fuller prescribed several heart medications, but my pains continued to get worse in spite of them. I asked whether another operation was an option. He said, "No, it would be too dangerous, and besides, we have no assurance that a third one would work any better than the first two."

Dr. Fuller insisted that I stop work. I had no argument with that, because I couldn't do my job anymore. Within a few weeks, in addition to my other medication, I was taking 20 nitroglycerin tablets a day trying to relieve the pain. Nothing helped for long. Once again I needed Gene, and he was there for me. I continued to worsen and soon became totally dependent on him. I couldn't leave the house. He had to do everything—shop, cook, wash clothes, do the housework and get my medicines. Despite our differences, he was a great friend and caregiver.

My need for nitroglycerin to relieve the anginal pain kept going up, from 20 tablets a day in 1978 to 100 in 1982. This pain would begin in the middle of the front of my chest as an oppressive weight that soon felt like it was crushing my breastbone against my backbone. From there the pain would spread to the base of my neck and then to both shoulders and down my arms. Nearly any exertion would bring this pain on—even brushing my teeth, going to the toilet, standing up, laughing, crying, or eating. I suppressed my emotions and barely reacted to anything. I was afraid to move. But the pain came anyway. It woke me every night, frequently more than once. I never knew whether I could get an hour's sleep or maybe two or three before this would happen. When I went to sleep, I often hoped it would be forever.

Gene was the only person I ever saw in the house. He watched over me like a hawk, despite the uncrossable ocean between us. There's no way I could've survived without him.

In every sense I was a prisoner in my own home. My heart pains were as confining as if there were bars on the windows and locks on the doors that couldn't be opened. There was no escape from this "death row," except by death itself. As I continued to worsen, I prayed for that final release. The thought of dying was no longer frightening to me; the thought of continuing to exist this way was.

The only time I got out of the house was when Gene took me to see Dr. Fuller every six weeks, or when he'd have to call the ambulance to take me to Blodgett because the pain wouldn't go away after six or eight or even ten nitroglycerin tablets taken within five to ten minutes. Gene would follow in his car and wait until I'd been admitted before going home. He had to do this every few weeks throughout the period from 1978 to late 1982. Each time I'd be in the coronary care unit for several days, on infusions of heparin to prevent clotting and nitroglycerin to increase the blood flow, until the pain stopped and my condition stabilized. All told, I made that trip about 50 times, and each time I left home I thought, "This is the end. I won't be coming back." But somehow I survived. On four of those occasions, Dr. Fuller did angiograms to try and clarify what was going wrong. He found that my grafts were closing down and the disease in my coronaries was getting worse. After the last study, he told me all the grafts had closed.

I became deeply depressed and asked over and over, "Why me? Why don't I just die like Dad and John instead of hanging on like this?" I continued to pray that God would take me. Waiting for the last moment was agony.

Dr. Fuller never quit trying. In the fall of 1982 he learned of a promising new drug called Procardia that might help me. But at that time, this agent was being tested in only a few research centers. Nonetheless, Dr. Fuller was determined to get it for me, as I had nothing to lose. Anything was better than continuing the way I was. He made many calls to the right people in the pharmaceutical world and wouldn't take no for an answer. Finally they gave in and sent him a supply for me. Within days after he started me on it in mid-November of that year, I could tell I was better. Though it didn't relieve all of my heart pain by any means, I didn't have to be rushed to Blodgett anymore.

Most important, my favorable response to this drug encouraged Dr. Fuller and Dr. Delavan to reconsider whether another operation was an option for me. After much thoughtful deliberation, they concluded that it was. This was very good news because it meant I could have a meaningful future if the operation was a success. Dr. Delavan assured me he'd find some good veins in my thighs for use as grafts. In addition, he said that there'd been significant improvements since 1976 in both the heart-lung machine and the techniques he'd use to protect my heart while he was implanting the new grafts for me. I asked how many three-time operations he'd done. "Three," he said.

I quickly replied, "Let's make it four." No question, I was elated to have this chance.

Dr. Delavan opened my chest for the third time on March 5, 1983 and searched my thighs for veins. He needed every inch of the segments he could find to make three grafts to bring new blood supply to my heart. The operation was long and difficult. Then, just after he'd closed my chest and thought he was done, my heart stopped. I went belly-up on them. They reopened my chest and tried everything to get it started, but nothing worked. In fact, things looked so bleak Dr. Delavan decided it was hopeless to go on. Just as he turned to go out of the room to tell Dee and the other members of my family that I was gone, my heart started to respond. Later he told me that I'd taught him to never give up. "I'm glad I could do this for you," I replied, and we both laughed.

My recovery was prolonged this time—30 days in the hospital. Every little thing that could go wrong did, but overall I could tell I was better. I went home thankful to God that I'd made it again and could feel improvement each day. Gene was there to help me as he'd always been.

After three months I felt ready to go back to work. But Dr. Fuller was concerned. "I can't okay your going back this time," he said. "The mental stress of nursing and the heavy physical effort of lifting patients will be too much for you. You need a medical disability pension, and I'll help you get it. I want you to live." I knew he was right and thanked him for his care and concern. After a few days of mulling over what I might do, I decided to move to Seattle because by then, all my children had located in that area.

When Gene and I talked about proceeding with our divorce, he said, "Take your time. You've stayed here this long, a little more time won't matter." As you can imagine, I didn't want to hurt him. He'd been a true friend, and I'll always be indebted to him for the wonderful care he gave me, but I couldn't remain married to a bisexual man who couldn't change his homosexual affinity. We obtained our divorce and parted friends.

With that behind me I was ready to leave. The next day Norm, my son, called. He lived near Terry and Jeff in Auburn, a small city about 15 miles south of Seattle, "Mom, I'll fly out and drive you back. We all want you here."

He came, and we loaded up a U-Haul and headed west to a new life for me. That trip was a ball all the way to Auburn, where we arrived after six fun days. Terry and Jeff made me feel right at home. I stayed with them in their pleasant mobile unit for the next month while I found a comfortable apartment in nearby Federal Way. Those early fall days were beautiful, and I quickly fell in love with the Pacific Northwest.

One of my first priorities after getting settled in was to find a cardiologist to take Dr. Fuller's place. I was lucky again. I found Dr. William Bilnoski—thorough, caring, and someone I could trust. I told him that I knew I could have further trouble in the future and said, "If my veins close again, please don't ask me to go through another surgery."

He looked at me and said, "I think that's a fair request. I really do. I'll never ask you to go through another open-heart operation." I knew he meant it.

I got along well for the next three years, until I had an

episode of severe angina in 1986. I thought my time had come again. But Dr. Bilnoski put me on the triple medical program of Procardia, Tenormin and nitro paste, and this enabled me to return to full activity with little angina.

I had a scare of a different type the next year. My apartment was broken into about 2:00 in the morning while I was asleep. I awoke with the sixth sense that someone was near. As my eyes adapted to the dark I could vaguely make out a large, shadowy figure towering above me only inches away. I could feel his presence and froze, with my heart pounding out of control. I was sure he was about to attack me. Seized by terror I screamed with all my force. My intruder was so startled that he turned and fled out the front door. Even though he'd taken nothing and hadn't harmed me, I couldn't stop shaking for over an hour and didn't feel safe until dawn.

After this episode, Terry and Jeff asked me to come and live with them again, and I gladly accepted their invitation. In retrospect, I really owe that midnight prowler so much because if he hadn't broken in, I wouldn't have moved. And if I hadn't moved, I would have never met the man who has come to mean everything to me. After moving back into Terry's mobile home community, I met Mrs. Anna Richter, who lived at the far end of our court. We visited a few times and talked about her beautiful flowers and her pretty daughter, who was 11. Later that year I went to San Bernardino and visited with Dee for several weeks. When I returned in October, I was shocked to learn that Mrs. Richter, though only 54, had died of lung cancer and been cremated a few days before. Strangely, I'd never seen her husband, a tool grinder for the Boeing airplane company, in the year and a half I'd lived there, though I'd often see his daughter.

In August 1989 we neighbors learned that Mr. Richter was

going to have an operation on the arteries of his right leg to help him walk. A few days after he came home, the little girl who lived next door came to me and said, "Patsy, I'm awful worried about Mr. Richter because his daughter says he won't eat and can barely get out of bed."

I decided I'd bring them some good home-cooked food that evening. I made up a pot of chicken and dumplings and baked a cake, too. I knocked, and the mysterious Mr. William Richter hobbled to the door and opened it. My eyes met his, and I haven't been the same since. There was instant chemistry between us. I can't describe it, but I knew it and so did he.

We began seeing each other and one thing led to another. In May of 1990 he asked me to go to Prague, Czechoslovakia, to visit his sister with him. I asked Dr. Bilnoski if I could travel that far, and he said, "Go!" We left in mid-June and came back at the end of July, after having a fantastic time. While we were there, the communist government fell, and there was dancing in the streets. Pope John Paul II visited, and we saw him from a distance. We were there while history was being made. It was wonderful.

Some may raise their eyebrows and say that Bill and I weren't "legally" married at that time, and they're correct. We still aren't. But I have a good reason for this. In the event I should become ill again, I wouldn't want him to be legally responsible for my medical expenses. If we were legally married, such an illness could take everything from both of us, and that would be unfair to Bill and his daughter.

We made personal history while there, too. We went to Prague's majestic, towering cathedral and at first just stood silently in the shadows of the vestibule, feeling a sense of awe. After a few minutes Bill took my hand and led me to a pew near the back where we sat down. He then said in a hushed voice, "Now is the time you tell me if you really love me." After we had spoken in whispered tones for a considerable time, we got up and walked down the long center aisle to the main altar, where we knelt and said what was in our hearts. We both said that we loved each other and would never leave one another. Then we turned and walked back down that long aisle, hand in hand. We had to laugh when we came out into the bright morning sunlight, we really did. We both felt like, "Oh, my goodness, we just got married!"

After we returned home, we found that our rent in the trailer court had been raised to $325 a month. We couldn't afford this. Since Bill owned five acres of wooded land way out in the country, about 85 miles south of Seattle, we decided to move our modest mobile home there. It was like heaven to have the beauty of nature all around us—wildflowers, rabbits and an occasional deer in the yard. Even though Bill had to drive an hour and a half each way to his work at Boeing, our lives were happy because we had each other.

Then late one afternoon in early March of 1991, Bill drove up very slowly and just sat there, unable to get out of the car. His face was ashen and he was obviously in pain. He had suffered a heart attack in 1985, and I knew he was either having another one or was threatening to do so. No matter what, he needed emergent care. I said, "Bill, move over, we're going to the hospital," and I drove him there, 22 miles, as fast as possible. After the emergency doctor checked Bill over, he sent him by ambulance to St. Joseph's Hospital in Tacoma, 40 miles away, while I followed in our car. I called Dr. Bilnoski, who came quickly from nearby Auburn and performed emergency angiograms that revealed severe obstructions in all of Bill's main coronary arteries. Dr. Lon Annest, a cardiac surgeon at that hospital, took him promptly to the operating rooms and implanted four grafts made from the veins in his left leg to bring new blood supply to his heart. Following that surgery, he did well and was discharged nine days later.

I hadn't told Bill that in January I'd begun to have angina again. It wasn't severe at first, but by May I couldn't hide it from him anymore. By then I was taking 15 nitroglycerin tablets a day and was waking up at night in pain. Because I didn't believe anything more could be done, I didn't call Dr. Bilnoski for an appointment. But by late August I couldn't hold out any longer.

I saw Dr. Bilnoski in his office in early September. He said what I knew he'd say. "I need to do an angiogram."

I asked, "What good will that do?"

"I can't treat you blindfolded," he said.

I knew he was right and agreed to the angiogram, which proved to be the most difficult I'd ever had because of heavy scar tissue caused by the many previous procedures I'd had at both groins. Dr. Bilnoski had to push as hard as he could to insert the catheters through this dense tissue. For a time I just wanted him to stop.

After the procedure was completed, I was taken to the recovery room, to wait for word of what he'd found. About a half hour later when he walked in, I could tell from his downcast look that the news was bad. He sat down on the edge of my bed and, while holding my hand, said with a quiver in his voice, "I'm sorry, Patsy. Your grafts are closed. We have to talk about something."

By now tears were running down his cheeks. "I can't keep my promise. I can't let you go without a try. I believe you still have a chance."

I knew he was talking about more surgery. I said, "Where are you gonna find the idiot to try this? Who would attempt a fourth-time operation on me with no veins to use for grafts?"

"There is only one man in the world who can do this," he said, "and fortunately, he works at the Providence Medical Center in Seattle. His name is Lester Sauvage. He has developed several new operations for patients like you who have no veins. He uses the internal mammary arteries, which are soda-straw-sized vessels that run parallel to the edge of the breast bone, one on each side. They are harder to use than veins, but they last longer and work better."

"There's no way that he can do a fourth operation for me," I said.

"That may be so, but I'd like you to talk with him anyway."

"I'll go home and think about it."

Bill and I went home, and late the next afternoon the strangest thing happened. I was sitting at the kitchen table with Bill when the phone rang. A man sounding as if he were tired after a long day said, "I'm Dr. Sauvage, and I'm calling because Dr. Bilnoski asked me to review your angiograms and then call you. I believe we can help you. Could you come to my office?"

I thought, "Don't you have enough to do? Go call someone else!" I knew that I wasn't thinking straight so I just said, "May I call you back?"

He said that would be fine.

As soon as Dr. Sauvage had hung up, the phone rang again. This time it was Dr. Bilnoski. I said, "Well, it's about time you got around to calling!"

He laughed and said, "Now, Patsy, you said you would see him, and I really want you to do this."

So I said, "Okay, let's get this settled. I'll call Dr. Sauvage back and tell him I'll come in to talk, but I'm not promising any more than that."

When I called Dr. Sauvage, he was kind and gentle, but

firm at the same time. "I'd like you to come to my office next Tuesday morning," he said, "and be prepared to stay if I decide we can do the operation for you." There had been only one other person in my life who could talk to me like that: my father.

I was very apprehensive when I first opened the door to Dr. Sauvage's and his seven partners' large office. I thought I was going to meet a young surgeon who was eager to operate. Instead, he appeared to be in his late 50s or early 60s and did not look at all like someone who was anxious to open my chest. I was totally calmed by his peaceful appearance, quiet manner, and the air of confidence, competence and concern that he evidenced for me. No question he was intense, but I felt at ease with him. The beautiful crucifix on the wall in his personal office told me a lot about him. He asked what I thought about having another operation.

"Do I have a chance?" I asked.

"Yes, if you're willing," he said.

And then he asked me the big ol' question of why I wanted to live. I said I had to survive to take care of Bill. I also told him that life is so precious that I wanted every moment I could have. I told him I enjoyed living, I enjoyed laughter, I enjoyed people and, if it was God's will, I wanted to live as long as I could.

Dr. Sauvage said, "I think you'll do just fine. God has more for you to do in this life."

Those words gave me the confidence I needed and I said, "Okay, let's do it." After the admitting arrangements were completed, I went directly from Dr. Sauvage's office into the hospital with the secure feeling that I'd come to the right man.

The rest of the day was occupied with the staff getting me ready for my surgery, which was scheduled for the next morning.

Toward midnight when all was quiet, Dr. Sauvage stopped in on his late rounds, checked me over, visited briefly, and then said as he turned to leave that he was confident God would bless the work he and his team would do for me. Those words soothed my worries, and a short time later I dozed off.

I went to surgery at 7:00 A.M., September 18, 1991, with a sense of peace. While the surgery was complex, there were no significant problems. Dr. Sauvage used both of my internal mammary arteries in one of the special ways he'd devised to bring more blood to my heart. After my operation Bill said, "Dr. Sauvage took your heart in his hands, but he took all of us in his arms."

I did well and went home 12 days after my operation. There was no doubt I was better. I had only two complications, neither of them serious. My breasts were sore for about three weeks, and the lower end of my incision required about the same time to heal up.

The night before I went home, Dr. Sauvage and I spoke at length about the happy days that lay ahead of me. He was confident my heart would be okay, and that I'd be able to reach out to the world around me. Just before leaving he gave me the St. Francis of Assisi prayer and told me that reading it would refresh and invigorate me when I needed help. I read it many times during the first year after my operation, and then I gave it to my sister to help her when she was having trouble with one of her children. You read this prayer, you accept it, and it stays with you. It's like something my mother used to say to me—God never closes the door before He opens a window. But if your mind and heart aren't together, you may not see the open window. It's like when you're having a real horrible day and nothing's going right, and then all of a sudden something bright and beautiful comes along, but you can't see it because your eyes are closed. Well, I'm not that way. I will go with the beauty, the love and the music whenever they come. I've never been alone in my life; God has always been near. And when I found Bill, that was the proof of it all.

It's now a little over four years since my surgery, and I've never been better. Dr. Sauvage told me that my internal mammary artery grafts would stay open, and they have. I'm thankful for his research, which led to the development of the operation he did for me.

God invites us to do His work in this world while we're going by. Since my last surgery I've come to realize that He only asks us to do what's possible. I believe that if we find someone who really needs us, we should give him or her our best shot. Bill is that someone for me. I want to be needed as long as I'm here, and when I'm not needed anymore, I'll be ready for God to take me home. In the mornings when Bill goes by my room before I get up and says, "Well, we're here again," that's priceless. It makes me happy to arise each morning and say, "Thank you, God, for another day."

I learned that to be totally happy I must give—not 50 percent, not 75 percent, but 100 percent. If I do this, God will reward me with peace and joy.

Since my last surgery, I've become more aware of the beauty of life. I've become more tolerant. I've developed a deeper faith in God. My new life is more vibrant. I have a serenity now that fills my life with joy, and this is the miracle of it all. It does not bother me that there are no churches for miles around because out here in the country, I'm in the center of a gorgeous cathedral where I can talk with God at any time.

I'm so happy now, I have to tell everyone that the sun is brighter and more golden than it's ever been. I thank the Lord for the rain because it, too, brings life to our land. Every tree, every bush and every blade of grass is a gift. I see each flower as a bouquet arising from our earth in thanksgiving to God. The song of the lark in the meadow has a message that I perceive more fully than before. Everything around me is different now. It is so much more. It is the work of God.

I'm thankful I can wash the dishes now. I couldn't before. I'm thankful I can vacuum once again.

I look at my children differently. I look at them in wonder. Before, it was so easy to find fault. Now I don't. I'm here for them when they need me.

I've learned not to wait to say, "I'm sorry" or "I love you." I learned to say it today, while I still have time.

Comments by Dr. Sauvage

The danger of doing open-heart surgery for any patient increases progressively with the number of times that it has been done before. I was especially concerned about Patsy because this was her fourth time, and I had never done a fourth-time operation for a woman. Even so, I had a good feeling that my team and I could help her. Still, I was very apprehensive when I cut down the middle of her breast bone with the oscillating saw because I knew that the heart was fused to the underside of the bone by dense scar tissue. I prayed that I would not cut into it and cause uncontrollable hemorrhage.

Once we were past the critical danger point of reopening Patsy's chest, our next challenge was to find and free the delicate right and left internal mammary arteries that lay covered by scar tissue just to the respective sides of her divided breast bone. If these arteries had been injured in any of the three operations that Dr. Delavan had done, or if I were to injure them, we would have had to acknowledge defeat and close the wound without being able to do anything beneficial for

Patsy. The trauma of such a fruitless operation would have made her worse and could have even caused her death.

My strategy to restore an adequate supply of blood to Patsy's heart depended on the internal mammary arteries being in good condition, since all of the veins that could be used as grafts had already been employed in her three previous surgeries. No suitable artificial graft was available at that time, and there still isn't one today. (Developing such a graft is one of my long-range research goals.) But we were in luck—Patsy's internal mammary arteries were of good quality, and I was able to free these vital structures from the chest wall without injuring them. I knew then that we could help her.

Before that day when my wife and I interviewed Patsy and Bill for six hours on the porch of their mobile home, far out in the country on a warm spring day, I knew only her complex medical history. Early in the course of the interview I asked Patsy about her teenage years. With that question, she suddenly became silent and pensive. When I asked what was wrong, she broke into tears. Mary Ann and I were stunned. Then, after a few minutes when she was able to speak again, she said, "It'll be hard, but I'll tell you everything." And she did for the next five hours.

We came to realize in those hours that the emotional anguish of Patsy's personal life, from the time she was 15 on, had been even more traumatic for her than the four open-heart operations she subsequently had to undergo. In the course of her life, Patsy has been where few people have had the misfortune to go. Her vibrant spirituality helped her to overcome the emotional and physical adversities that beset her during the period of 1950 through 1991, even though she was nearly overcome by the apparent hopelessness of the dark days from 1978 to late 1982. But once there was a chance for success, her spirit bounced back and helped carry her through to renewed health. She came through my surgery for her on September 18, 1991 with flying colors.

Patsy did well after her operation until Monday, the 30th of October 1995, when she was suddenly struck down by a major heart attack while visiting her sister Dee in San Bernardino, California. She was rushed to the nearby Loma Linda University Hospital (where she had worked from 1962-1971) and admitted to the coronary care unit. Four days later when her condition had stabilized, angiograms were performed which revealed that the internal mammary grafts which I had placed were excellent. Instead, her problem had been caused by acute obstruction of a coronary artery on the back side of her heart. The Loma Linda cardiologists opened this vessel by stretching the blocked channel by inflating a tiny balloon which they had passed into this site—a procedure called "balloon angioplasty." But the passageway quickly closed again and Patsy's condition suddenly became very precarious. The cardiologists worked rapidly and within minutes reopened the vessel by placing an expandable metal stent across the narrowed area to maintain the flow pathway. At the time of this writing, three days after the procedure, the vessel continues to function.

I have spoken with Patsy via her room phone in the Loma Linda coronary care unit, and have found her spirits to be buoyant and her wit to be sharp. Yet, she is a realist and knows that her time could be short if the stent fails. Patsy is joyful despite this present adversity because her spiritual vision is clear. She knows that God will be with her through all of her days—no matter what. Patsy has the wisdom to appreciate that eternity with God is her ultimate destiny. Because of this she accepts the will of God in all things, including the length of her earthly life.

We've Got to Share
to Really Live

Marshall McLachlin

Hi! I'm Mac. I started poor and have had to work for everything I've ever had. I was born the second-youngest of five in St. Elizabeth's Hospital in Yakima, Washington, on May 31, 1925. My parents were apple farmers and had come to Washington from Vermont. Unfortunately, in the Depression years of the early 1930s, they couldn't sell the fruit and lost the farm to the bank in 1933. To this day I can still see those foreclosure people pulling my mother's sterling silver set right out of her hands. She loved that silver, and I can hear her crying, "No, no, you don't get this! It's mine! It's mine!" They took it anyway, along with everything else.

We had nothing left and moved into a run-down little house in Parker, a nearby town of 200 people in the lower Yakima Valley, where I went to school. My father couldn't get work. Few people could in those days. FDR was president, and when the Work Projects Administration (WPA) came in, Dad worked with a hand-shovel building roads. In the spring and summer, Mother worked in the fields and orchards, and in the fall she sorted and packed fruit and vegetables in the warehouses.

As a boy I worked as a farmhand whenever and wherever I could, sometimes making ten cents an hour and glad to get it. When I got all the way up to $.25 an hour, I was in clover. To make $2.50 a day after ten long hours in the hot sun was something. When I was 12, I made $8.00 a week carrying water to the pickers in the peach orchards, and would cash my check in Jack's Place, a poolroom in Wapato that Dr. Sauvage's father owned. He was a gentle man who always took time to talk to me when I came in. I couldn't go in the back where the gambling was, but I could eat at the lunch counter in the front and get a good meal for a quarter. My experiences in those early years taught me the value of work, and at the same time they've enabled me to appreciate the panic that people feel when they lose their jobs and all they have.

As a child, my wife, Nadine, went to St. Peter's Catholic Church every Sunday in Wapato, the same church the Sauvage family attended. She often saw "Boy Blue," as Dr. Sauvage was called when he was little because of a sailor suit he wore, and his sister, Coco, with her Shirley Temple curls. Nadine still remembers the exquisite hats their mother wore, a different one for each occasion. Mrs. Sauvage had a real presence as she prayed and kept watch on her children.

When I was 11, I lost the vision in my right eye as the result of an accident while playing with a friend. We were banging sharp sticks together, pretending they were swords, when suddenly the end of his broke off and flew into my eye. After several months, when I became adjusted to having only one good eye, I vowed that this would never hold me back, and it hasn't.

When World War II came along in 1942, I tried to join the army but couldn't because my blind eye made me 4F. I still wanted to serve my country, so I found another way. Though only 16, I dropped out of school and joined the army transportation corps. For three years I worked on a big freighter carrying supplies to Alaska and Hawaii. When the war was over in 1945, I wanted out. Instead, they transferred me to the army air corps and made me a diesel engine instructor. After a few months, I got to know everything there was to know about those engines and taught my students how to take them apart and put them back together. Though I enjoyed doing this, I wanted to go home. Finally, after 18 months they discharged me, and I went back to Wapato to restart my life.

All I wanted was a chance to work and make something of myself. I bought a truck with my savings from the army and started a business hauling hay from the valley to the coast. Though I wanted to make money and grow, I knew that doing it this way would be difficult. But it was an opportunity, a beginning, and that's all I asked. I lifted thousands of those heavy bales of hay, loading them into boxcars all afternoon and into my truck in the last of the daylight hours. At night I drove 170 miles over the mountains—remember, there was no I-90 in those days—to General Mills in Tacoma, where I unloaded, turned around, drove back, got four hours sleep, and started another day. True story. It was hard work, 20 hours a day, but I was getting ahead.

In 1948 my sister, a nurse at St. Elizabeth's, arranged for me to meet Nadine, a beautiful nurse with whom she worked, by inviting us to Sunday dinner at her home. It was instant love for both of us, and after a whirlwind courtship lasting only a few months, we were married. Following our marriage, I continued to work hard as ever, but I soon decided that there had to be a better way to take my bride up and beyond to greater things.

We saved every cent we could, and in 1950 we moved to Seattle, where we hoped to build a better future for ourselves. I sold our truck and bought a gas station. That was something—it was ours! Nadine worked at Providence Hospital while I worked from 5:00 in the morning to 8:00 in the evening washing and undercoating cars, repairing engines and pumping gas. No one in town gave better service or worked harder for his customers. We were getting by and saving money. But our gas station days came to an abrupt end when the projected path for the new freeway was determined to pass right through the middle of our property. It didn't seem fair, but we couldn't stop progress. We looked around and saw an opportunity. We used the money from our station and bought an auto spring shop. Before long I added chassis parts to our line of springs and went from one gas station to another to see if we could supply their needs. Business began to increase, and I knew that if we could expand our product line we could go places.

Our big chance came when we had the opportunity to purchase the Seattle branch of a large automotive-parts warehouse chain. Nadine and I put everything we owned on the line with the bank and took the plunge. With much hard work and a lot of good fortune, our business grew and prospered. We incorporated, named our company Mar-Lac, and have become one of the largest auto-parts warehouses in the Northwest, with branches in Seattle, Spokane, and Portland. Today we employ 200 people, carry more than 250,000 individual part numbers, and make an $8 million inventory available to our customers. None of this has come easy. In our earlier years I worked 12 to 14 hours a day, while Nadine worked just as hard as wife, mother and nurse. What we have accomplished we have done together. Until the past two years, I worked ten hours a day, six days a week, and loved every minute of it.

Maybe it's because I've had to work for everything I've ever had, and maybe it's because I love my country, that I get so upset with the people who take advantage of our system of government. The S&L frauds, the foreign lobbyists, the political action committee payoffs, and the people who don't pay their taxes really get to me. I pay what I owe and it's a lot, but I'm thankful that I live in a country where I have been able to do what I've done. The tax cheats who rob the system on this end and the politicians who do it on the other should all be put in jail.

More important than our financial success has been the blessing of our three children—Marsha, Bruce and Baby Dale, who died at 11 months of cystic fibrosis. Losing our baby was very hard on us—especially for Nadine, as she was in the sanitarium with tuberculosis when he died. Somehow our faith in God got us through that awful period. Nadine was able to come home after a year and has been fine since. The joy of our lives has been our children and now our five grandchildren. I believe they are what life is all about.

When I look at the epidemic of broken homes and the number of children who don't get the attention they need, I realize how unstable the future of our society really is. I'm convinced that a child who does not receive love in the first few years of life will likely be screwed up forever. The human brain is a lot like a computer. If its basic circuits are programmed wrong, it can't function right. The windows of opportunity to make the connections for joy and peace come early and don't last long. Children who have been abused or even just plain ignored don't have much of a chance. We are the product of our early environment. That's why a mother's work is so vital to the future of our world. There's no greater profession than shaping the minds and hearts of the children of today because they'll be the adults of tomorrow who'll run the world.

My parents couldn't give me money, but they gave me something that is far more valuable. They gave me love and affection. Mom, Dad and the army also taught me how to work, and so did the Depression. You have to be responsible for what you do. Don't blame someone else. Look in the mirror and you'll have it right. I've been responsible for taking care of my employees and running the company so they can have a job and take care of their families. I told our children, and I tell our grandchildren, "Give life the best you have, and be true to yourselves and to each other."

I have always loved the outdoors, and I've climbed some big mountains—the Grand Tetons, Mt. Rainier, Mt. Hood and Mt. St. Helens. I jogged, fished the high streams, and thought that nothing could stop me. Then one morning in 1980 it hit me. We were at our farm on Whidbey Island when suddenly, I had a crushing pain in my chest and trouble breathing. Nadine knew what was happening. She put me in the car, caught the ferry and rushed to the Providence Medical Center in Seattle, where Dr. English, a cardiologist, performed X ray studies of the arteries of my heart that showed I was about to have a major heart attack; the blood supply was blocked.

Dr. English said bypass surgery had to be done as soon as possible. I asked for Dr. Sauvage, because I knew of his expertise, and Nadine recalled him from her childhood. Even though by that time it was late at night, he was in the hospital and came quickly to see me. I'll never forget how he sat on the edge of my bed in Room 504 and assured me that my life after the operation could still be a full and productive one. Even so, I was skeptical and afraid, but his quiet confidence gave me the courage I needed to go ahead.

But I was still scared. You'd better believe I was. When you get the word that they're going to open your chest, lift your heart up and hold it in their hands while they work on it, you suddenly look at your life very differently. If you hadn't appreciated each day before, you certainly do then. In that short span of time before I went to surgery, I realized I was having my first real brush with death, and if I didn't have God with me, I might not wake up. When I did awaken afterward, I was thankful to be still alive.

I got well quickly and went home after a few days. My strength came back rapidly, and I was soon charging ahead once again at 80 miles an hour and wanting to do more.

No question the surgery helped my heart, and no question the whole experience helped my soul, too. I believe that a special grace from God went through my surgeon and into my soul when he held my heart in his hands. Before I left the hospital, Dr. Sauvage and I had several discussions about the spiritual side of our lives that made me stop and think. Though I was not a religious man before my operation, once home I began to think a lot more about God, the value of each day, and what made me happy.

When I returned to work, I tried even harder to help my employees. I found that when I made them happy, I was happy, too. It made me feel good deep down inside. Life had been wonderful before, but now it seemed even better. Our business continued to grow, our employees were happy, and Nadine and I were finding great joy in our lives.

Life was a bed of roses until 1985, when I had a stroke. I had just stepped out of the shower one morning when suddenly, my left side wouldn't work: I couldn't make a fist, I couldn't touch my nose, I couldn't hold a towel, I couldn't put my pants on. I hollered for Nadine. Again she knew what was happening and quickly dried and dressed me. Then she helped me get in the car and drove to Providence as fast as possible.

I was scared of death, scared of becoming an invalid, and scared I was going to die. But again Dr. Sauvage, with God's help, brought me through. He obtained an arteriogram, which showed that cholesterol debris from the artery in the right side of my neck had broken loose and gone up into my brain and caused the stroke. He took me to surgery and cleaned this material out of my artery. After the operation, I recovered full use of my left side and within a few days went back to life as before. Once again I'd had another brush with eternity, and the Almighty took care of me.

Meanwhile, the company was growing and making money. Owning your own business is a special responsibility because a lot of people depend on you for their living. In a sense, our employees are an extended family to us. The company is much more than an inventory and some machinery. Most important, it's a collection of human beings, each with his or her own wants, needs, hopes and dreams. I've got to be their leader. To me it's like a rope; when you pull one end, the rest follows. But if you try to push the rope, it curls up. People won't go when they're pushed. The Russians found that out. You have to lead; you have to pull the rope.

I know all the people who work for us in Seattle and most of them in Portland and Spokane, too. I make a point to call them by their first name and take every opportunity to talk to them. To me they're Ed and Tom and April. To them I'm Mac. I'm not Mr. McLachlin. Whenever I see a new employee, I walk right over and say, "Hi, I'm Mac. I work here, too." You ought to see the difference that makes! When they see me sweeping the floor or straightening the stock on the shelves, they keep the warehouse cleaner. After all, if I don't care, why should they? When they see how much I care, they care, too.

Even though you start out small, you'll grow if you do what's right. That means you have to work, you have to be honest, and you have to understand that every person is important. Some people never learn these basic facts and wonder why they're left at the gate. They want to take and never give. It can't be all one way. You have to share. You have to give back.

In 1989 I started to get tired and out of breath from doing things that shouldn't have bothered me. Within a few weeks, I was really bad. Dr. Sauvage was afraid that the graft to my heart was closing, but Dr. English performed angiograms that showed it was still perfect. The trouble was a new blockage, but fortunately one that could be fixed by placing a tiny balloon in the narrowed area of my coronary artery and then inflating it to widen the channel, a procedure called angioplasty. Dr. English did this difficult operation, and it worked. This was my third brush with mortality, and I suspected there'd be more, but I was okay again and thankful to be alive and well.

I was fine until early 1993, when Nadine and I took a trip to the Grand Canyon to see its awe-inspiring scenery. I got very tired there, much too easily, and felt short of breath. I thought things would get better after we got home, but instead they got worse. A lot worse. Soon I couldn't go up even one flight of stairs without having to stop halfway up and catch my breath for a few minutes. When I walked from the office to my car at the end of the day, I'd collapse in the seat and have to wait for ten to 15 minutes just to get strong enough to start the motor and drive home. And once there I'd have to sit for another several minutes before I could open the door, get out, and walk slowly into the house. Soon I couldn't sleep at night because I'd get so short of breath. Nadine knew that things were bad and getting worse, but I was stubborn and refused to admit she was right. I couldn't accept that I was going down again. But when it got so I could barely walk across the room, I gave up and called Dr. Sauvage. He said, "You must see Dr. English today," and he promptly made arrangements for me to do this. After a brief examination, Dr. English sent me straight to the hospital where he began urgent medical treatment to relieve the congestion of my lungs. In these past several days, the medicines have helped, and I'm considerably better now. My breathing is easier, and I'm a good deal stronger.

Dr. English hasn't told me for sure yet, but I know I need another operation—this time a new valve. Yes, I'm scared, but I have the courage to accept what comes, because I believe in God. I've been doing a lot of thinking these past few days about my life and how lucky I've been. I've tried to do my best. I'm content, because God knows I've given life all I've had. I'm going to pull through this, too. I want to live. I don't want to leave Nadine. She needs me, and I sure need her.

Before we stop, Dr. Sauvage has asked me to tell you what's in my heart of hearts. Happiness is in my heart, even though I'm down again. Happiness is a state of mind, you see. It's not a physical thing. It's not the car you drive. Happiness is your family, your neighbors, your friends, and your employees and their families. Happiness is kindness; happiness is sharing; happiness is caring. Happiness is love for others—that's what happiness is all about. When you help others, you find happiness and get closer to God. We've got to share—and share—and share—right to the end, to really live.

Comments by Dr. Sauvage

Though he convalesced slowly, Mac eventually did well after his second open-heart surgery, which I asked my partner, Chris Davis, to do for him. He replaced Mac's aortic valve with an artificial one and also bypassed a blocked coronary artery with a new graft. This was a scary time for Mac and his family and for me, too, as I was very concerned about him. Dr. Davis did a great job, but he and I both knew that, at best, Mac's recovery would be slow. After his operation, I told Mac it would take him at least three months to regain his strength and not to worry, that this would be slower than following his first open-heart surgery 13 years before. Mac needed encouraging words in those early weeks when he was progressing slowly. Fortunately, my prediction proved accurate—he was better after three months and back to normal after six months. He continues full of vim and vigor now, three years later.

Since his first surgery, Mac and I have been close friends. He is a person you can always count on, and he is generous almost to a fault. I believe he would give the shirt off his back to someone in need.

Mac is a member of The Hope Heart Institute's board, and I am the director of research. He works tirelessly to promote the Institute and raise funds to help support its many programs. And he does this the old-fashioned way. He leads by example.

Mac and his wife and children give large sums of money each year to support these investigations upon which lives depend.

In addition, each year Mac and I have fun working together on a fundraiser for The Hope Heart Institute with the Seattle Mariners American League Baseball Team. On that night, they let me throw out the "celebrity" first pitch, and that's a big deal for me. This past year we raised $95,000 to support the Institute's research, and they clocked my pitch at 58 miles per hour, right down the middle. Next year we hope to raise $100,000 at this event, to help defeat heart disease in our time.

Mac's son, Bruce, runs the company now, and he is doing a great job. Mac still assists with broad policy decisions and makes annual visits to selected dealers to whom they supply auto parts in Washington, Oregon, Idaho and Alaska. His visits are good for the business and good for him, too. Mac is a splendid person who is finding joy in his retirement by continuing to do what he has always done—helping those who need him.

Never Give Up

June Baldwin

My story starts back in old St. Louis, where I was born November 16, 1926, the third of five children in a religious family. Mom, a devout Catholic and member of the Third Order of St. Francis, looked after us, and Dad, a bricklayer, provided for our needs. Mom always tried to impress on us that we had to work harder to succeed in life because we were black. She told us over and over that we had to get some kind of diploma because nobody could take *that* away from us.

I grew up like other working-class black kids in South St. Louis. Our neighborhood was pretty much integrated and we kids played together, even though we went to our own segregated schools. Even then I remember questioning why the color of my skin should determine where I could go to school and what I could do. But that's the way it was, and there was not anything I could do about it. In 1944 I graduated from high school, and that fall I enrolled in Stowe's Teacher's College, an institution for blacks only.

Early in my freshman year at Stowe's I met Joe, who was home on leave from the coast guard. After being discharged three months later, he returned and swept me off my feet. When he gave me a diamond ring, I thought that I was really in love and said "yes." Mom was unhappy because she did not trust him and wanted me to stay in school. But my mind was made up. I knew she was wrong! Nonetheless, she had a big wedding for us in May of 1945 at St. Mary's Church. I was excited and happy, but not for long.

I soon realized that Mom was right. Joe was a scoundrel—mean, moody and abusive. Worse yet, he got even meaner after our daughter, whom I named June, after me, was born a year later. It got so bad that I was afraid to close my eyes while he was awake. I feared for my life and my baby's. Only when I knew that he was asleep in the bedroom would I dare to doze off on the couch in the living room.

There were times after he'd hit me in the face and bloodied my nose that I wanted to kill him. In fact, I got scared that I might actually do this. Finally, I couldn't take any more and got a lawyer to get a court order to keep him away and to start divorce proceedings. By early 1947 I was divorced with full custody of my nine-month-old baby. I was then barely 20, alone, hurt and afraid. The task of raising my infant daughter seemed overwhelming and would have been, except for Mom's help. She was always there for us when we needed her.

Then a few months later something wonderful happened. I met Lafayette Baldwin. He was tall and stood out in a crowd.

Lafayette was one handsome man. The first time we went out together, he called for me in his stylish old Packard and took me to a movie. That shiny black car was really something: four doors, big fenders and a tall trunk on the back.

Lafayette, who was 15 years older than me, accepted my past and was kind and considerate to my baby and me. He was so special that I was soon in love with him, and two years later we were married on June 11, 1949. Our love has held us together now for 47 years, many of which, since 1980, have been difficult, due to my long periods of illness. Our only child together, a daughter, was born in 1954. We named her Frandelia after my sister and both of my grandmothers.

When June was 11 and Frandelia three, I saw a notice in the *St. Louis Post-Dispatch* advertising for applicants to the Board of Education school for licensed practical nurses. This seemed like something I could try to do. I talked to Lafayette and Mom and they both encouraged me to apply. Since Lafayette worked nights at the Buster Brown Shoe factory, he said that he could look after the children during the day while I attended class. I applied and was very happy when my application was accepted, even though I'd been out of school for 12 years and knew I would have to learn how to study all over again. But this was my chance to become a nurse, help sick people, and be somebody. Also, there was the practical matter of money. We needed a second income to be able to send June to a Catholic school and, in three more years, Frandelia, too.

I worked hard, got good grades and enjoyed my studies, especially when I began to take care of patients. After graduating in 1959, I was hired as a staff LPN in the emergency room of the black hospital in town. Then, after the racial barriers started to come down, I got a job in the emergency department of the prestigious Jewish Hospital that was located out near big old rambling Forest Park, where we often took the children for picnics on Sunday. A few years later, when I was offered a position in their new intensive care unit, I gladly accepted it because I wanted to take care of the critically ill patients. This was a big step up for me, and I was proud to have that important responsibility.

With Lafayette working nights and me working days, we could send the girls to private schools and take good care of them. June grew up to become a beautiful woman and went on to college at UCLA, obtaining a Bachelor of Fine Arts in Design. Following graduation, she moved to Seattle, where she has been very successful in her career as an interior designer. In addition, in her early years she was in demand as a model, often abroad. June was very generous and invited me to accompany her on several trips to faraway places, where I'd get to see her model the latest fashions. I especially remember our going to Paris, London and Tokyo. After her work was over, June and I would take an additional few days to tour about, see the sights and meet new people. Those trips were memorable times.

Frandelia, who is just as beautiful as June, has had a different but equally exciting life. She married LaRue, a journeyman sheet-metal worker, when she was 18. Because the employment opportunities were better in Seattle than St. Louis, they moved there in 1980. She and LaRue have had a loving marriage now for 24 years and have five wonderful children, ages 23, 18, 13, eight and six. I believe they have been and continue to be a happy family due in large measure to Frandelia's staying home and taking care of the kids.

My physical troubles started deceptively in the late 1960s. At first my right calf would only cramp a little after I'd walked a half-mile or so. I thought this little ache would go away, but instead it gradually got worse. Finally, after about two years, this cramping in my calf had progressed to the extent that I could barely go the length of the intensive care unit at the hospital before I would have to stop and rest. At that point I asked my supervisor to assign me only patients who were close to the central nursing station. She agreed, and in that restricted area I was able to give my patients excellent care. In fact, I did more than my share of the unit's total work.

In addition to my nursing activities, I got involved in the hospital's labor union politics because there were still a lot of injustices that affected the lower-echelon work force of all the hospitals in St. Louis in the 1960s and 1970s—poor pay, long hours, no representation and no job security. The majority of those affected were black—essentially all of the housekeeping staff and about 60 percent of the LPNs and ward secretaries. In 1971 I volunteered to lead a drive at the Jewish Hospital to recruit these groups for the teamsters' union.

I thought I had it done in 1972, when the hospital agreed to an election. But a week before it was to be held, I was called into the nursing office and told by the supervisor, "We no longer need your services." I was fired just like that! She said it was because I could no longer do my job. That was a lie, and she knew it! I loved my patients and could still take good care of them. But she had been ordered from above to get rid of me because of my activities on behalf of the union. There was nothing else she could do. With me gone, the election was cancelled.

Fortunately, aided by my union connections, I didn't have any trouble getting a good position at the teamsters' medical clinic in central St. Louis, and I worked there for the next 13 years. It was an excellent place—better pay, better hours, and we workers had a voice. Also, I didn't have to walk as far in the clinic as I'd had to walk in the hospital.

My leg didn't worsen very much through the rest of the 1970s, and Lafayette and I enjoyed our life together. After a lot of years, we changed churches in 1979, switching from the Catholic parish in our neighborhood to the nearby Baptist church because the minister there and I had been friends since our days together in grade school.

In 1980 my leg, which had been tolerable for a little more than ten years, suddenly got much worse. Instead of being able to walk a block before the aching in my calf would force me to stop, now I couldn't go 50 feet before this would happen. My limitation had abruptly become so severe that there was now no way I could continue working. At this point the clinic doctor sent me to a surgeon who injected dye into the vessels of my leg and took X rays (a procedure called an arteriogram), which showed that the arteries were blocked in my thigh and behind my knee. He said I had to have vascular surgery.

I didn't want an operation, but by then I was afraid I'd lose my leg if I didn't. Just the thought of an amputation made me shudder. I had taken care of many amputees, and I remembered vividly that few of them ever walked again. Also, I had to work because Lafayette's income at the shoe factory was not enough; we needed my paycheck, too. There was no choice—surgery had to be done. The surgeon took a vein from my leg and used it as a bypass graft to carry blood from the open artery at my groin to the open vessel below my right knee. Everything went well, and I recovered rapidly. The new blood supply that flowed through the graft into my lower leg made it like new. Within a few weeks I went back to work and felt so good that I thought nothing could ever put me down again.

But I was wrong! In 1984 my calf began to bother me again when I walked. The hurt was mild at first, but by the next year this distress had worsened to the point that it seriously interfered with my ability to work. At that time I was 59 and eligible to retire on Social Security. When the clinic doctor advised me to take that option, I did so.

In the next few months, Lafayette and I talked a lot about where we wanted to spend the rest of our lives and came to an important decision. We decided to go west and moved to Seattle, Washington, where June and Frandelia and her family lived. Being near our children and grandchildren was what we wanted most.

After we found an apartment and settled in, I was able to get along so-so with my leg for a couple of years by limiting my walking to about a half-block at a time. If I tried to go much farther than that, I'd have to stop anyway. Though this wasn't good, I could manage. But then my leg went bad, real bad. I didn't have to tell Lafayette; he knew. It was St. Louis all over again. Before long I could barely walk across the room. I went to a surgeon who, after he had performed an arteriogram, told me that the graft in my leg had closed off. Worse yet, he said that the disease in my arteries had advanced markedly and blocked nearly all the channels below my right knee. I asked him if I'd lose my leg. He said I would if I didn't have surgery, and soon.

Once again I had no choice. I had another operation—a new graft. But this time it helped for only a few months. Then my calf started to cramp again whenever I tried to walk more than a hundred feet. Within days I was more limited than ever before. As this was happening my foot became ice cold, and when I went to bed, it would soon start to pain. This hurt would either prevent me from going to sleep, or if I had been lucky enough to doze off, it would quickly awaken me. My big toe developed a sickening ache, and before long the skin behind the nail became very dark and broke down to form a deep ulcer. The doctor said I had to have more surgery. I did not know where to turn; there seemed no other way. He took me to the operating room again, but this time it did no good— not even for a little while.

By then my right foot was hurting all the time, a deep, burrowing ache that intensified when I lay down to try and get a little sleep. But I couldn't stay in bed for even an hour because my foot would hurt so much that I couldn't stand it. I took Tylox pills, one after the other, but they only dulled the pain a little; it was always there.

The ulcer over my big toe continued to get bigger. Horrified, I watched it grow and felt its searing pain. I couldn't walk and had to get around in a wheelchair. When Lafayette took me to the clinic, I sensed from the look on the doctor's face that he feared for the worst. I knew it when he said, "There's nothing more that I can do. I want you to see Dr. Sauvage. If anyone can save your leg, he can."

I grasped at this ray of hope and asked, "How soon can I see him?"

"Tomorrow," he said.

That night Lafayette held my hand while we prayed for a miracle—that Dr. Sauvage would be able to stop the pain, heal my toe, save my leg, and let me lie down and sleep for a few hours. But the next afternoon our hopes were shattered when he told us that more blood vessel surgery wouldn't help, and that my leg should be removed because it was holding me prisoner in my wheelchair and, in time, would kill me. He said that if I had an amputation I would be able to walk on an artificial leg. Though I heard the words, I couldn't accept his advice. He said that he understood my fears and would try to help me make this difficult decision.

In the weeks that followed, my agony worsened as the ulcer of my big toe relentlessly extended upward onto the top of my foot. There was no relief from the pain. I couldn't escape the hurt. The only thing I could do to reduce it even a little was to sit up day and night. The single change in my morbid weekly schedule occurred on Tuesday afternoon when Lafayette took me in my wheelchair to see Dr. Sauvage, who would examine my foot, renew my prescription for pain pills, and try to help me accept the necessity of having my leg removed. But just thinking about being a cripple terrified me. I couldn't face this grim prospect alone. I had to lean on Lafayette even more. He was as he had always been—kind and considerate—and he did all he could to help and encourage me. I couldn't have continued without him.

As the ulcer of my foot continued to enlarge and deepen, I was at the same time getting heart pressure whenever I tried to move, and sometimes I got this even when I was quiet. At that point the infection in my foot began to spread rapidly up the front of my leg, and I became feverish. Dr. Sauvage quietly insisted that my leg had to be removed immediately. I couldn't resist any longer and signed the consent form. A few hours later an orthopedic surgeon amputated my right leg two inches below the knee.

I came through the operation okay, but an hour later I had a heart attack in the recovery room. My blood pressure was low, and the doctors had to work hard to save me. Several days later Dr. English, my cardiologist, performed angiograms of the blood vessels of my heart, which showed that they were all either narrowed or closed. The disease process that had taken my right leg was also attacking my heart, but for a time the awful pressure on my chest stopped.

My amputation stump healed slowly, and two weeks after my heart attack I was sent home in a wheelchair; I was too weak to use crutches. Poor Lafayette, who was then 78, had to do everything—shop, cook, keep house and dress me—but he never complained. The hope that I could one day walk on an artificial leg and take care of both of us kept me going.

But a few weeks later my hopes were shattered again when my remaining leg began to go bad—ice cold and painful with discolored toes—even worse than the way my right one had started. I could see myself without legs, condemned to a wheelchair for the rest of my life—helpless. The terror of this mental picture was overwhelming. To make matters even worse, the pressure on my chest had by that time returned and was increasing by the day.

The marked decrease of circulation to my left lower leg alarmed Dr. Sauvage so much that he performed an arteriogram to see if it was possible to successfully implant a graft to bring more blood to my foot. After seeing the X rays, he didn't think this was feasible because not only were all of my main arteries closed, most of my small ones were, too. There appeared to be no suitable vessel to which a graft could be attached at the far end near my foot. Not only would such an operation most likely fail to save my leg; Dr. Sauvage was afraid that the stress of surgery would also cause my heart to stop. He told me later that he didn't know what to do because there seemed to be no solution for my mounting problems.

While Dr. Sauvage waited, I watched in horror as the skin over my big and middle toes became black and hard. Over the next few weeks, this dead skin broke down to form deep ulcers that continued to enlarge and hurt even more. Once again this ache forced me to sit up day and night. I cried for sleep and took more pain pills, but the agony wouldn't go away. In addition, when I tried to move, the pressure on my chest became so severe that I could barely breathe. I was being hit from all sides and feared that I would soon die.

In spite of my fears, I refused to give up and gained strength to fight on from Lafayette, family, prayer and friends. My old minister and members of his congregation in St. Louis called and were a great help. So were my two sisters in Cleveland and my brother and sister in St. Louis. Dr. Sauvage also gave me courage when he told me that he, too, was praying for me. We were in tune with each other, and that established a bond between us that no one could take away. I knew he would be with me all the way, no matter what.

As my foot worsened, Dr. Sauvage realized that he would have to do something soon or I would lose my last leg. Because he knew I would chance anything to avoid being confined in a wheelchair for the rest of my life, Dr. Sauvage decided to risk all and try to bring more blood supply to my foot, for it was either that or amputate. I was ready and anxious to proceed, despite knowing full well I might die on the operating table, or that I could still lose my leg even if I survived the surgery.

Dr. Sauvage took a very long vein from my leg and used it to carry blood from the big artery at my left groin to a tiny artery that he found near my ankle after a tedious search. Somehow my heart held up through all of this and the operation was successful—the graft brought more blood supply to my foot—enough to stop the pain and start the healing process. After closing the wounds, Dr. Sauvage removed my big and middle toes because they were too far gone to save. With the improved circulation, my foot healed up and didn't hurt anymore. And once again, for a time, my heart stopped hurting, too. I could now go to bed and sleep! God had heard our prayers, and Lafayette and I were very thankful.

But my problems were far from over as a few weeks later, the squeezing pressure on my chest returned. Before long this pressure would strike me even when I was just sitting in my wheelchair or lying in bed. Soon this vise-like grip around my chest would awaken me at night, too. I thought, "First my right leg, then my left, and now my heart—where will it end? What will be left of me?" I knew that if my heart wasn't strong enough for me to stand, I could never wear an artificial leg and be able to get out of my wheelchair to take care of our apartment. And if I couldn't do that, I knew I'd never realize my dream of someday surprising Lafayette by preparing his dinner, something I hadn't been able to do for a long time.

As my heart continued to worsen, even little things like brushing my teeth began to cause the squeezing pressure on my chest. But this was nothing compared with the crushing pressure caused by the ordeal of transferring from my wheelchair to the toilet. Because of this and my fear of not being able to get back to the bathroom in time, I spent long hours in that little room just reading my Bible and praying that I would get better soon.

It was now apparent to Dr. Sauvage and me that I needed surgery to increase the blood supply to my heart. Perhaps it was a premonition—I felt that I'd be all right because I had lots more to do in this life. Dr. Sauvage said God has a plan for all of us and that my most important work could still be ahead of me. When he told me that he had scheduled my heart surgery, I wasn't afraid.

My family and friends rallied around me again. Early in the evening the night before surgery, my old friend, the minister from St. Louis, called and prayed with me. Much later, Dr. Sauvage, on his rounds near 1:00 A.M., stopped in and briefly checked me over. Turning to leave, he said, "I'm sure God will bless our efforts for you." Those words once again made me feel at peace, and I went to sleep.

The next morning Dr. Sauvage used the two small arteries from inside the front of my chest, one from each side of my breastbone, to bring more blood to my heart. During my operation the people from my old church in St. Louis had a prayer-line going for me. I came through the surgery without any trouble and went home ten days later.

The night before I left the hospital, Dr. Sauvage came to my room and we talked for a long time about the days that lay ahead of me. He was optimistic and said I'd be able to do God's work here on earth for many more years. Just before leaving he gave me a St. Francis of Assisi prayer card and said that it was a favorite of his. Since then this prayer has become a favorite of mine, too.

I did well for the next two years, but then I had a scare. I had to have another operation, this time on my neck to keep me from having a stroke. Dr. Michael Zammit, one of Dr. Sauvage's protégés, repaired the last open artery going to my brain and, by the grace of God, everything went fine.

It is now just over five years since my heart surgery, and my life has truly been renewed. I rarely have chest pressure anymore, and what I have isn't much. I can walk with my artificial leg and even go upstairs, though the end of my stump bothers me some. It's a blessing just to go to bed and enjoy a good night's sleep. I see life much differently now. Before my many troubles began, I used to think more about me; now I think more about others. One of the great joys of my new life was to see the happiness on Lafayette's face when I finally surprised him by cooking his dinner. There I was, standing by the stove, telling him to sit down so I could serve him. He was so proud of me! Neither of us will *ever* forget that moment.

I've come through a lot, and I'm the wiser for it. Though I stopped smoking many years ago, if I could relive my life, I would never start in the first place, for I now know that doing so contributed to the development and progression of the terrible disease in my arteries.

I wonder—if I'd never had any problems, would I be happier than I am now? I doubt it. Each day has become more precious to me. It wasn't always so. I didn't fully appreciate my health when I had it. I didn't realize the priceless value of just being able to get up and walk until I became a prisoner in my wheelchair. I didn't cherish being able to sleep until I couldn't. Now I thank God every morning for the rest He has given me and for waking me up to a brand-new day. I don't take life for granted anymore. It's a sacred gift, and I'm thankful for each day.

I learned that happiness is what life is all about and that this comes from loving my family, helping people and talking to God. Just looking at His world makes me happy. I love to see the green leaves come forth in the spring, mature throughout the summer, turn brilliant colors in the fall, and then detach and flutter back to the earth, one by one. Since my many illnesses, I've come to appreciate even more the beauties of nature that are all about us, from a flower in the garden to a cloud in the sky.

I take insulin now for my diabetes, but life is still a ball. Summer before last, Lafayette and I flew to St. Louis in June and had a great time visiting my brother and sister and our old minister and his congregation. We came back to Seattle in July to be here when our great-grandson was born. Imagine that—me, a great-grandmother! When the excitement of that special event settled down, we went to Alabama to be part of Lafayette's younger brother's 50th wedding anniversary, which was quite an affair. It's hard to believe that our 50th is getting close—in fact, just three years away.

The year we were married, Lafayette promised that someday he'd take me to Hawaii. And later this year he's going to do it. When I was so sick, I never thought I'd live to see the day.

My many illnesses have taught me to trust in the Lord and to never give up. I gain great happiness from speaking with all the people who call and say, "Just talking to you makes me feel better." I tell them that if we have faith, God will see us through any suffering, and I also try to convey this message to everyone I know.

I don't fear death anymore, for I know that God will take care of me. When my time comes I'll gladly go, but until then I'll be happy here. There's still so much that Lafayette and I want to do.

Comments by Dr. Sauvage

As I look back on my care of June, I realize that I nearly waited too long to bring new blood supply to her remaining leg. I was afraid she would die if I did additional surgery. Thank heavens her determination to live and walk again finally gave me the courage to move ahead with her care before it was too late.

After that operation, June not only had to have surgery to bring new blood supply to her heart, she later had to have an operation to bring more blood to her brain. Despite all of this, June now finds joy in each day as she walks on her artificial leg and takes care of Lafayette.

The disease process in June's blood vessels, called hardening of the arteries, has in the past 30 years progressively blocked the flow of blood not only to both her legs, but also to her heart and brain. Plaques have developed in the walls of the arteries throughout her body because of abnormalities in her blood chemistry, including elevated low density lipoprotein cholesterol (LDL); decreased high density lipoprotein cholesterol (HDL); high triglycerides (fatty acids); high blood sugar due to diabetes; high fibrinogen (blood protein that forms clots); and sticky platelets (cell particles that cause clots). Though plaques such as these narrow the channel inside arteries through which blood flows to the tissues, they seldom completely close this passageway. In most instances complete closure occurs when the diseased walls of an artery cause the blood in its narrowed lumen to clot. This is the event that finally blocks off the rest of the channel and stops the flow of blood to the tissues downstream that had been supplied by this artery. In June's case, this loss of blood supply has been so extensive and so severe that it has caused her to suffer marked impairment of function, severe pain, and death of several parts of her body (right leg, a portion of her heart, and two toes of her left foot).

June is living proof that even severe diabetic patients who are afflicted by widespread arterial disease can do well for long periods with modern care if they—and their doctors—don't give up. And she has taught me an important personal lesson, too. I have learned that when my life gets hard and disappointments abound, to think of her courage and optimism and keep trying. June's life is a clear statement that we haven't lost until we give up.

I Accept God's Will

Anna Gnecchi

My twin brother died when I was one hour old, and the midwife told my father I wouldn't live the day. But somehow I survived and six weeks later, in 1904, my parents took me, with little else to their name, and emigrated from Austria to America. They settled in the northwest part of the United States, in Seattle, Washington, where I've lived for the past 92 years.

I grew up in a poor but loving home and progressed through school. When I was 12 I asked a girlfriend, "Who is that boy with the beautiful brown eyes?" She said, "That's Carl, your teacher's little brother." I said, "Oh, I'm going to marry him!" I swear, that's what came out of my mouth, even though I didn't know him or anything. If my father had heard me, he'd have been furious: "I'm sending you to school to learn, not to look at boys," he'd have said. Yet I was right, because 12 years later Carl and I were married, and we had 60 wonderful years together before he died.

In our early years we lived on $15 a week in a tiny house with my mother-in-law and Carl's brother, Hugo, and his wife. Carl always worked hard, and eventually he became a repair expert for and later part owner of the Northwest Optical Company, while I stayed home and took care of the house and our five children.

I had no health problems until my left hip started to pain me when I was 55. At first it hurt only after I'd walked several blocks, but over the next year or two the distance got shorter and shorter. Finally, my hip hurt whenever I bore weight on it or moved. Soon it ached at night, too—a throbbing pain deep down in the bone that prevented me from sleeping. I held out for 12 years, till I couldn't stand it any longer. Then Dr. Callahan, my orthopedic surgeon, replaced my worn-out arthritic hip with an artificial one. What a relief! For the next five years I had no pain and could walk as far and as fast as I wanted. It seemed like heaven just to be able to walk and sleep again. Dr. Callahan sent many of his patients who needed that kind of surgery to visit me, so I could "show off" and inspire them to have the operation.

Then, when I was 72, I had a major setback. It happened while I was running to catch a bus that was just about to pull away. As I tried to jump onto the step before the door closed, I tripped on the curb, plunged forward nearly under the left front wheel, and landed full force on my replaced hip, where I felt the bone snap. The pain was so intense that I knew something terrible had happened. I was taken by ambulance to the Providence Hospital, where Dr. Callahan found that the impact had broken the attachment of the bone in my thigh to the artificial replacement. He operated the next day and did all he could, but from that time on my hip hurt constantly. There was no relief.

After that injury I was in agony whenever I moved my hip. The whole area pained like someone was opening and closing a pair of scissors in my flesh. Dr. Callahan had to reoperate on me seven times over the next few years. Eventually, when I was 77, the wound became infected and for the next eight years I had yellowish-grey, smelly pus draining from a hole over my hip that grew to be as big as the palm of my hand and went down into the bone. There was so much drainage that Carl had to use several Kotex pads for my dressing each morning, so it wouldn't have to be changed until he could do it again in the evening.

Because of my many surgeries, my left leg turned in and was two inches shorter than my right leg. I couldn't bend the hip or knee. The only way I could get around the house was with my walker, and when I went outside I had to use my wheelchair. Still, I could do quite a few chores around the house during the day, and I read a lot in the evenings.

Some days the sickening ache in my hip would be especially bad when I'd make our bed. When that happened, I'd sing some of the songs we used to sing in the choir. "Ave Maria" and stuff like that. Real loud. It would help me through the worst moments. It was quite awhile before Carl, who at that time of the morning would be working downstairs in his shop, finally caught on and asked, "Are you singing because you're in pain?" I had to say, "Yeah."

Our home had two levels, a main upper one that opened from the street and a lower one that opened out onto the yard behind the house. These floors were connected by a steep flight of 14 stairs that became increasingly difficult for me to navigate as my leg got worse. Carl put up a special steel handrail to help me, and I soon learned to go down those stairs backwards, hanging on to the rail with both hands, and to climb up them on all fours, like a monkey. This worked well until my heart started to fail when I was 83. Then a trip up or down the stairs would completely exhaust me, take my breath, and cause me to feel faint. I was afraid of falling and breaking my good hip. I knew if that were to happen, I'd be a total invalid rather than just a partial one.

When my regular doctor told me my heart was giving out and that special tests were needed to find out what was wrong, I said "okay." After Dr. English, the cardiologist, performed my heart catheterization, he told me I needed open-heart surgery because my aortic valve leaked badly and my heart didn't receive enough blood supply. I said, "Well, I want Dr. Sauvage, because he operated on Hugo, and I've heard him being paged so often when I've been in the hospital for my hip that I feel I already know him."

But actually making the decision to go ahead with the surgery was something else. Some of my friends said, "At your age, why bother?" At first I wondered, too. But after a lot of prayer and thought, I decided to have the operation for two reasons. First, I wanted to live longer to be with Carl and our children and grandchildren. Second, I wanted to be better so I wouldn't be such a burden to them. I thought, "If I die on the operating table, then the Lord wants me now, but if I don't, He wants me to continue doing my job here for Him." That seemed fair enough. I was not afraid either of impending death or continued life, and went to surgery accepting God's plan for me, whatever it might be.

When I awoke after surgery, Dr. Sauvage was standing by my side. I did very well, much better than anyone expected. I remember how surprised Dr. Sauvage was on the second night after my operation, when he came to see me on his late rounds about 2:00 A.M. and found me sitting up in bed enjoying the early-morning hours reading a novel. He smiled and asked, "Is it a good story?" I said yes and told him that I read like this at home nearly every night.

There's no question my heart surgery has helped me. Dr. Sauvage replaced my aortic valve with one from a pig and brought new blood supply to my heart. Now whenever I see a picture of a pig, I have a special feeling of friendship because of that little part that makes it possible for me to live.

I regained my strength after several weeks and was able to go down the stairs hand over hand, and then crawl back up without feeling faint or even getting short of breath. Just being able to do that again was wonderful. I can still do it now, nine years later, though a bit slower because I'm older. If I were big and heavy, I couldn't climb them at all. I'm fortunate to be small and only weigh about 100 pounds.

A year after my surgery, Carl died of heart failure. The days after his death were hard and lonely. For weeks it seemed impossible that he was gone, for we had been together for so long. But I accepted God's plan for us and knew I had to adjust. In those early days after Carl went to heaven, I often talked to him. In fact, I still feel his presence and frequently speak to him now, especially in the early-morning hours when I'm with my books. I'll stop reading, and in my mind, we'll just visit for a while. I know Carl is with God and that someday soon we'll be together again. I'm ready when God wants me, but in the meantime I'm thankful for each additional day of this life, too.

I often wonder why healthy people complain. I suppose it's because none of us fully appreciates our health until we've lost it. I have a friend who said, "I don't know how you can be happy being so old and crippled." I told her that I have my down moments, too. Everyone does. But most of the time I'm happy just to be here. I accept God's will.

Celesta and her three children came to live with Carl and me 25 years ago after she divorced her husband. At first we took care of her and the children, but in recent years, and especially since Carl died, she has been taking care of me. With Carl gone and the children long since away, it's just Celesta and me at home now. She goes to work long before I get up. While she's away, I do the little things that I can around the house, so it will look nice when she returns in the late afternoon. I never watch television in the daytime; there's too much else to do, and besides, there's not much that's worth seeing. But there are a few good programs in the evening that we enjoy together. After Celesta has gone to bed, I hobble over to my big chair near the fireplace, say my prayers, and settle down to read for several hours. I thank God that my lens implants work so well. Even though my leg and age restrict me, I can travel around the world in my books, all in one night if I want to. I generally finish reading about 4:00 A.M. and go to bed. I don't need much sleep and get up between nine and ten o'clock in the morning.

Celesta had to take over dressing my hip after Carl died. This was hard for her at first because there was so much foul drainage, but she got used to it and did a good job. After a few months, though, my hip got worse, and I had more pain due to a deep infection that couldn't drain out. The doctors were afraid the infection would spread to the pig valve in my heart and kill me. They recommended radical surgery. I said, "Do it!" One year after Carl died, Dr. McDermott, who'd taken over Dr. Callahan's practice when he retired, took out the upper half of the bone in my left thigh plus the artificial hip that was attached to it in order to remove all the infection. The wound healed, and for these past seven years I've had no drainage and little pain. But my left leg is now four inches shorter than my right, and each time I put any weight on it, the thigh bone that remains pushes up and shortens my leg still more. At my age and with my shortened leg, I couldn't live alone. I love it here with Celesta, and I'm thankful that she takes care of me.

Celesta worries a lot about me when she's at work, despite my telling her not to. If I listened to her I'd just sit while she's away. I know her concern is because she's afraid I might fall and hurt myself. But I've got to try and help, even though she scolds me gently when she finds on her return that I've scrubbed the kitchen floor while she's been gone. I know that deep down inside she's proud of me for doing what I can. I'm good at scrubbing on all fours, and I've got plenty of time to make that floor shine. Being old like I am, there's not a lot left that I can do. But what I can do is very important to me, even if it isn't much. I want the kitchen to look clean and fresh for Celesta when she comes home in the afternoon. Moreover, the exercise keeps me from getting stiff. Celesta knows there's lots I want to do before I die and that I may not have much time left. I can't count on tomorrow. I've got to use today while I have it. I'm never bored; I don't have room for that. One of my remaining projects is to make a family photo album for each of the children. I've completed Celesta's, but I've four more to do. If I work hard, I can complete one every six months. I hope I've got enough time left to finish all of them.

I like to work for our church. Years ago I helped with the school lunch program, but I can't do that anymore. Now I send get-well cards to the parishioners who are sick. Receiving such a message from the oldest parishioner probably makes them smile and feel better.

My advice to older people is, "Don't feel sorry for yourself because that won't bring you happiness. If you do, you'll get depressed, and there's nothing worse than that. When you wake up in the morning, just think of all the good you can do that day, and you'll be off to a good start. Even if you can't get out of the house or out of bed today, you can still be happy." There are months when I don't get out of the house except on Sundays, when Celesta or Doris or one of my other children takes me to church. They're all so good to me and would take me wherever I wanted to go, but I like it here at home.

Though I'm a very happy person at 92, Celesta and I can talk about my approaching death without being morbid or depressed. We both recognize how fortunate I am that my spirit is vibrant, even though my body is old and getting weaker. We are realistic and appreciate that death is part of life. In some measure, we've both come to know the reality and the beauty of life, of death, and of what lies beyond.

I often think about how the young people of today are on their way to becoming the old people of tomorrow. This occurs in so gradual a way that one hardly realizes that it's happening. But one day, they, too, will ask, "Where have those precious years gone?" and in God's time, they will move on to eternity, the same as I will have done long before them.

When Carl died eight years ago, I had to face the question of whether I wanted to live or die. I chose to live, but I'm ready to leave whenever God calls me. As St. Francis says, "It is in dying that we are born to eternal life." Until then I'll continue to do my best and be happy here. When you're my age, you can't have it better than that.

Comments by Dr. Sauvage

Anna has a special place in my heart because to know her is to love her. From the time I first met her, I have known from the sparkle in her eyes that she is a happy person despite her age and infirmities. At 92 she has it all together and loves life with a passion. She starts each morning by thanking God for giving her another day. She sees herself and all about her as maintained in existence by the power of God. This is reality to her.

Anna accepts her limitations and does what she can. She learned long before I performed her heart surgery nine years ago that happiness comes from doing God's work in this world, and that this can be as simple as saying "good morning" with joy to Celesta. Though she misses Carl greatly, she knows that he is with God and that both God and Carl are with her spiritually.

I believe Anna has a message for all of us at any age, but especially for those in their retirement years. She tells us that while life here is good, what follows in eternity can be vastly better. Anna helps me realize that we *are* spiritual beings in human form, having an amazing earthly experience.

Catching the Dragon Killed Me

Billy Coons

I was on heavy drugs and died when I was 32. The medics brought me back, though I was unconscious for three days and on a breathing machine. The truth is—dying was the best thing that could've happened to me at that time. If I hadn't died, I wouldn't be alive now. I'd reached bottom; my life was a shambles. I couldn't go lower. But by the grace of God, I've returned and regained my life.

Now let's go back to the beginning, and I'll tell you how it all happened. I was born in Seattle on May 15, 1956, the second of four children. Both my parents drank too much and paid little attention to me. I needed them to hold me tight and tell me that they loved me, but they didn't have time—Mom with her endless tasks around the house and Dad with his work as a meatcutter. My self-esteem was low and I thought the other kids were better than me. I went through Little League baseball with a friend and his father. My dad was too busy.

I started drinking beer and smoking marijuana when I was in the sixth grade. Before long one thing led to another, and in time I got to the heavy stuff. Doing this seemed okay to me because everyone I knew did it. Drugs were the "in" thing to do and easy, too. There was no trouble getting them from the dealers around school. Taking them made me one of the crowd.

I left home when I was 15 and moved into an apartment with my girlfriend, who was also on drugs. I never got a high school diploma, though I went until my senior year. Sad to say, I was largely illiterate. The system just moved me along whether I worked or not, and would've graduated me if I hadn't dropped out to try and join the army toward the end of the Vietnam War.

The army turned me down because the examining doctor said I had a grade-three heart murmur. I didn't know what that meant. I wasn't sick or anything, but he said I should see a specialist anyway. The first one I saw was kind of old, and the next year he retired. After that I saw another one. Both of them said my aortic valve was too small and leaked a lot, and this was causing my heart to get bigger and bigger. The second specialist recommended surgery, but I wasn't interested.

By the time I had left high school I was addicted to cocaine. I still remember my first high after I snorted the real thing, but that wonderful feeling of "catching the dragon" didn't last long—only a few minutes. Soon it was replaced by a desperate drop to the bottom. My mind craved the high, so I snorted again, but each time there was less high and more low. I

couldn't control myself. I couldn't sleep. Alcohol and marijuana put me to sleep, but not cocaine. I knew a dealer who
was awake for a week. I didn't want food. I only wanted to
"catch the dragon" again, but this became harder and harder
to do. I snorted more. In those early years I thought taking
drugs was smart. Only much later would I learn that they were
a one-way ticket to my own death that would take me away
from all that could've been good in my life. As time went on
I was spending thousands of dollars a year to get high, every
penny I got, any way I could. I was investing in my own
misery, and I didn't realize it.

When I was off drugs I was an excellent auto mechanic and
able to earn a good living. But in my addicted state I couldn't
repair anything, let alone my life.

I broke up with my first girlfriend after living with her for
seven years, and then I took up with another woman, who also
drank and drugged. We pulled each other down.

Year after year I got worse. Finally, when I was 25, I hit
bottom and nearly died. The police put me in a rehab hospital, where I stayed for 33 days. My withdrawal from cocaine
was a terrible ordeal in which I climbed the walls for days.
After what seemed like forever, my uncontrollable craving for
that high began to slowly decrease. Gradually, I got to where
I could survive without my fix. But I still had the desire when
they let me out, and even now I sometimes feel it, too.

Following my release from the hospital, I was clean for a
few months, but then I tried "just one snort." I wanted more,
and soon I was hooked again and falling fast. On my way
down I met Betty, a drugger and a drinker, and married her
when I was 28. We drugged and drank together, and before
long I was in free-fall. At 32 I hit bottom again. My life was
a wreck. I had no hope. I was back where I'd been seven years

before. Though I hated who I'd once again become, I was helpless and couldn't do anything about it.

I remember the day it happened—the 15th of October 1988. I'd just come home and sat down at the table to eat a cold, day-old hamburger when I suddenly felt faint and everything went black. The next thing I remember was feeling the cool air on my face while I was being transferred by ambulance from the Harborview Emergency Medical Center to the heart-surgery service of the Providence Medical Center. I had absolutely no recollection of the four days in between.

Later they told me I lost consciousness and slid to the floor, half under the table, after my heart stopped. Betty saw this happen and quickly dialed 911. But because we lived in a torn-up part of town, the medics had a hard time finding us. They took a wrong turn at the bridge and had to come back. I was far gone when they arrived. After starting CPR, they shocked my heart seven times to get it going, moved me into the aid car and rushed to Harborview, where I was admitted to the intensive care unit. All along they were forcing oxygen into my lungs to keep me alive.

No one could say exactly how bad my brain had been dam-aged by lack of oxygen during the time my heart was stopped. The doctors didn't think I'd recover, since my pupils were big and didn't get smaller when they shined a bright light into them, and I made no effort to breathe. By the morning of the third day the staff had given up on me because I had shown no improvement. They planned to disconnect me from the respira-tor that afternoon and let me die quickly, since they thought my brain was already dead. But somehow it wasn't, because toward noon I began to breathe on my own and show other signs of waking up. By midafternoon I was so much better that my nurse disconnected me from the respirator. Over the next few hours I continued to improve, and by evening I was wide awake and coughing on the tube in my windpipe. My nurse removed it. Since the staff now felt that my brain would be okay, they made arrangements to transfer me in the morning to the nearby Providence Medical Center to have my heart fixed.

The first person I remember after getting to Providence was my nurse, Rachel. She said I'd be all right and that I was a very important person—me. At that moment I needed all the encouragement I could get. Rachel was an angel at a time when I needed her the most. And when Dr. Sauvage came to see me, he made me feel important, too—like I was his son. He told me that the outlet valve on the left side of my heart had to be replaced because it didn't open enough and could not close. He said these mechanical problems had caused my heart to become very large and liable to stop, especially if I took cocaine. Dr. Sauvage then talked to me about drugs. He asked me to promise him that I'd never take any of them again. At first I thought he'd make me like new, and I could go back to drinking and drugging. But after we talked several more times, I began to realize that there'd be no purpose to my having the operation unless I stayed clean. I promised him that I would. But inwardly I didn't know if I could. This fear plus the thought of being cut open terrified me.

Dr. Sauvage then talked to me about the good I could do in the years ahead and how happy this would make me and him, too. I didn't understand most of what he said, but it made me feel better anyway because he was talking about what I'd be doing after my operation. He made it sound as if I had a future. I was still frightened, but a little less so.

After I had been at Providence for six days, they took me to surgery, where Dr. Sauvage stopped my heart, replaced my aortic valve with an artificial one, and then started my heart up again. By the third day after my operation I could walk easily, and four days later I went home. The night before I left, Dr. Sauvage and I talked some more about my future. Toward the end of our conversation, he gave me a plastic card with the Prayer of St. Francis and asked me to read it often. In the morning I went home to Betty and the surroundings where I'd died 17 days before. Going there scared me, but I had no place else to go.

I returned to see Dr. Sauvage in his office several times, more for us to talk than anything else. He always had time for me. I wanted to stay clean, but I was afraid I couldn't with Betty drugging every night.

Each day got harder. I couldn't control that feeling. It was turning me inside out. I had to have that high again. When Betty snorted that night, I did, too. It was wonderful. I wanted more. But after another few minutes my heart went wild and began to beat faster and faster and harder and harder. My whole chest shook, and I thought my heart would explode. Death seemed near, but over the next hour my heart gradually slowed down. At that point, I was totally exhausted and couldn't think. Later, when my mind had cleared, I felt ashamed, alone and lost.

Even after that near-disaster, it was hard to say no to Betty's drug dealer, who kept hanging around the house trying to turn me on. Betty couldn't go straight, and I knew that if I stayed with her, I'd break again. We were both on edge and fought over everything. Betty became so disturbed she sued for divorce and had me evicted, saying that she was afraid of me. Though her stories were lies, the divorce was granted, and she got all I had—little as it was.

After that I had no money and no place to sleep. I was hurt, angry and despondent. I thought of home and wondered if

Mom and Dad would take me back. I hadn't even seen them for a long time and doubted that they could forgive me. Though afraid, I went to see them anyway. When Mom saw me, her face lit up and she hugged me. Dad did, too. When I asked if I could come home to live, they said, "Of course." I realized then that they still loved me, despite all I'd done. I cried for joy and moved back into my old room.

At that time I still thought booze was okay for me because it was legal and so many people used it. Somehow I didn't get the message that this stuff was poison for me, too, until I was arrested for drunk driving a few weeks later and kept in jail for five days. This was the fourth major event telling me time was running out on my life. I didn't get it when cocaine nearly killed me when I was 25. I didn't get it when cocaine killed me when I was 32. And I still didn't get it when I had to have open-heart surgery ten days later. But after my arrest I finally began to get the message that I didn't have much time left to change my ways. Maybe it was Mom's prayers that did it. And Dad's, too. Though I'll never know the answer, I do know I couldn't have made progress in regaining my life without them.

The struggle to live instead of just existing has often been difficult for me in these past eight years, but I'm winning this battle for my life. The beginning was the hardest. I had to pick myself up and take the first step toward God. But once I did that and realized I could do something for myself, the next step became easier. I took a class in anger management that has helped me avoid making crazy statements and doing things I'd be sorry for later. And I attend AA regularly. This organization has helped me stop drinking—one day at a time. It's easier now. I'm going to literacy school twice a week at night, so I can learn to read and write well enough to compete for jobs. I'm even learning to type. Soon I hope to learn how to use a computer. Imagine that—me!

I'm proud to say I'm now off all drugs, including alcohol, and it's great to be free. I have energy again, and I enjoy my work, my friends and helping people. In my drug days, I had no ambition, went to bed about 9:00 in the evening, and didn't get up until late in the morning. I had nothing to live for but the artificial and bitter make-believe world of drugs. Now I want each day for what it is—a chance to improve myself and feel good. I get six to seven hours sleep at night, and that's plenty. I've got lots to do. On drugs, each day was a monotonous struggle to get through work so I could go home and get high to escape from life. No change, day after day. I was in a dungeon of my own making; I couldn't face real living and had to hide from reality. Now after coming home from work, I often walk along the beach or around the lake before going out for dinner with a friend. I've walked more in the past four years than I ever did before. Sometimes I walk over to the church and climb up the stairs to the lookout post and watch the sunset. Seeing that beauty helps me feel the majesty of God.

When I was on drugs I felt very much alone. But now, even when people are gone and no one's around, I'm not alone. I have God, Who loves me and will look after me. I've come to know that the spiritual part of my life is most important, and this has enabled me to break loose from my past. My escape was possible because of what has happened within me.

I can't go back and change my past. But I can learn from my mistakes and try to go forward to a better life. There's no sense pounding myself for what I've done or haven't done. Today is where I am and what I have. Life is like a stairway going up. I can't jump five steps. I have to take them one at a time. If I try to go too fast, I'll mess up. I've got to be patient.

When I feel those lonely times coming on and doubt that I can do the job, I tell myself I'm okay and ask God for His hand to lead me through the day. This is working because I'm doing better. Although I'm making progress, I'm still not safe and probably never will be. I know that I could break at any time, and this scares me.

Sometimes I want to go out and get drunk. Then I think, "What good will that do? I'll have the same problems after I sober up and more, too." I know that running away from my problems will only make them worse. I've got to face them, pray for help, and live one day at a time.

I took drugs because I was afraid of life. Now I get my high by living life, facing its challenges honestly, and doing something for someone when I don't have to. Helping Dad in the yard and Mom in the house makes me happy. I love to visit with my 96-year-old grandmother and then go out and cut her grass. It makes me feel good to do a perfect job for my auto- and truck-repair customers and see how happy they are when I charge them less than I could.

It's hard to listen. When drugs controlled my life, I heard very little of what was said to me. I'm doing better now. I've found that just listening can help someone who needs to talk about their troubles. I've found I don't even have to have an answer. All I have to do is listen, make a suggestion if I can, and let the person talking know I really care. Telling these people that I'll pray for them brings us together and helps, even though I can't solve their problems. I pray for my uncle who has cancer. I pray for my parents. I pray for my grand-mother. I even pray for people who've died.

Attitude is nearly everything. I used to say, "I can't do that." But I'll never know until I give it a go. Now I try to work to my potential. It's not important whether I finish first, in the middle, or dead last. What's important is that I give life every-thing I've got. If I do, I know I'll be happy. This attitude is helping me make the best of the rest of my life. It really works!

We all make choices in our lives. I've made a lot of wrong ones in mine, but I'm more on track now. I could've stayed dead and gone to hell, but thanks to a lot of people who cared, I've come back to life—real life. They gave me a second chance, and it's my turn now to help others. I want to tell them what I've learned so they won't make the mistakes I've made.

You have to learn to forgive. It was hard for me to get where I could forgive myself. I couldn't believe that God could still love me after all the awful things I'd done. But I've since learned He does and always will. If He could love and forgive me, then I had to learn to love and forgive myself. Only when I could begin to do that could I begin to do the same for others.

I know the odds are against me because few druggers can stay clean. But with God's help I will. I will! *I will!*

Comments by Dr. Sauvage

At the conclusion of the banquet at which I received the Seattle First Citizen Award in 1992, Billy came up through the crowd to the head table and gave me a rosary that I have carried with me since that time, a period soon to be four years. This gift is very special to me. Each day when I put it in my pocket, I ask God to help him stay off drugs. I can only imag-ine how difficult his struggle has been and continues to be. But he is winning this battle for his life.

When Mary Ann and I went out to Billy's parents' home in North Seattle to interview him, we were impressed with the clarity of his personal insight and the depth of his understand-ing of the difficulties he faced. We were deeply moved by his story and could feel the anguish that "catching the dragon" had brought on him. We hope that others who have fallen will listen to his words and be inspired to win their lives back, too. Billy needs our prayers so that he may continue to grow and never return to the hellish nightmare of the drug world.

Billy took the wrong road early in life and has suffered greatly for it. I wonder whether I would have been able to take a different route had I been subjected to the same temptations and troubled times that he was. In that vein I am reminded of the Biblical statement that may be paraphrased, "But for the grace of God, there go I."

Billy now takes life one step at a time and asks God to lead him through each day. He is a courageous man, and I'll always be grateful to him for my rosary.

"Come Quickly!
We've Got a Heart
for You!"

Chuck Medici

I was starved for sleep, but I couldn't lie down or I'd suffocate. I could eat very little and continued to lose weight.
Food had no taste. I had little strength left and could do
almost nothing.

Many people whom I'd known in Gig Harbor, Washington,
where we'd lived for the past nine years, didn't recognize me
anymore because I'd become so haggard and wasted. I felt
terrible, and knew that death was near.

Close friends would say, "Can't they do something to help
you?" and I had trouble saying that there was nothing more
the doctors could do. I told them I could only wait, probably
a month or two, or whatever, and then it would be over. With

sadness in their voices, they'd say, "We'll keep you in our prayers," and with tears in their eyes, they'd give me a hug.

I was 63 and dying of heart failure from a distended, weak heart that pumped much of the blood it received backward into my lungs through a leaky valve. I'd had my first heart attack when I was 37, my second when I was 48, and developed nearly fatal heart failure when I was 53. After my weakened heart had stabilized, I had a quadruple coronary bypass operation to increase the blood flow to my heart because my own vessels were largely blocked. Following that bypass surgery, I took medical retirement from my stressful job as service manager for GTE in Southern California after my cardiologist, Dr. Richard Taw of Santa Monica, advised me to do so because he couldn't get my elevated blood pressure down as long as I continued working. Some months later, Arlene, my wife, and I decided that, since we had lived in California all our lives, it was time for us to relocate and start anew somewhere else. Because I had visited the Northwest and loved the natural beauty of the whole western Washington region, we moved there in the spring of 1980 to Gig Harbor, a picturesque little town nestled in the evergreen covered hills on the shores of lower Puget Sound. A few months after we had settled there, Arlene started a children's daycare center, which in time would become our chief source of income. For the next eight years my heart held up fairly well, and I was able to help her run this facility, which we called "Small World Daycare." During that time I was cared for by Dr. David Clark, an excellent cardiologist, in nearby Tacoma.

But those happy days came to an end in February of 1989 when my heart, which had been failing insidiously, finally enlarged to the point where the inlet valve on the left side began to leak severely. This leakage then caused me to develop one episode of life-threatening heart failure after another. Each time this happened, the blood backed up into my lungs and forced liquid into the air passages, making it nearly impossible for me to breathe. As these passages filled with this sticky water, I had to gasp for air and fight for each breath. This mixing of air and water produced a whitish froth that choked me as it filled my windpipe, throat, nose and mouth, and blocked the passage of oxygen into and carbon dioxide out of my blood. Somehow during these near-drowning experiences, as I approached the portal of death, I would start to slowly improve, and over several hours recover to face the grim prospect of dying another day. I lived in dread of when that next attack might occur because when it did, I knew that I would struggle to breathe until it seemed I could struggle no longer.

During many of those crises, I'd have to be rushed by ambulance to St. Joseph's Hospital in the nearest city, Tacoma, where their dedicated emergency staff would prop me up and by dint of excellence and persistence manage to pull me through by applying tourniquets to my extremities to reduce the volume of blood coming back to my lungs, giving me powerful drugs to force my kidneys to put out water, and forcing oxygen into my blood through a pressure mask over my face.

On three occasions after I was breathing better, Dr. Clark asked different heart surgeons in Tacoma to repair or replace my leaky valve. After they had evaluated me, each one declined to do surgery because I was so fragile and my heart was so bad. This left me with only one option—to go home and wait to suffocate again when my lungs would fill with fluid. As the days passed, these drowning episodes occurred more often, and each time this terrible experience left me weaker and more afraid. By fall there was no doubt that I was near death.

Although my condition seemed hopeless, Arlene refused to give up. She talked to a friend in Seattle who said she'd heard of a Dr. Sauvage at the Providence Medical Center who took very high-risk patients. Arlene called his office and made an appointment for me to see him the next Tuesday. But toward midnight on Sunday evening of that week I developed the worst heart failure I'd ever had and was rushed to St. Joseph's. I fought for breath all the way to the hospital and for many hours after I arrived there. After being near death for most of the night, I was finally able to breathe a little easier toward daybreak.

When Dr. Clark came in later that morning, after having been up with me till nearly 5:00 A.M., Arlene told him, "I've made an appointment for Chuck to see Dr. Sauvage at two o'clock tomorrow."

"I'm glad because there's nothing more *I* can do," he said.

Dr. Clark then arranged for my transfer that afternoon by ambulance to Dr. Sauvage's care at the Providence Medical Center in Seattle, 30 miles away. Shortly after being admitted there, I was taken to the cardiac intensive care unit where, a short time later, he came to see me. My fear was that he, like the previous surgeons, would consider me too far gone and refuse to do my operation. I was encouraged when he approached my bed and quietly said in a reassuring manner, "I'm glad you're here." But after checking me over he said he needed more information to decide if he could help me and that Dr. English, a cardiologist, would do studies of my heart the next day to obtain this information for him. Despite his inability to commit himself at that time, I felt a little better because he hadn't said no.

The next afternoon after these studies had been completed, Dr. Sauvage came and told me, "Your main coronary arteries are all closed, but the old grafts are perfect. The problem is that the left side of your heart is weak and stretched out of shape, like a balloon. This stretching has expanded the base of the inlet valve so much that it can't close. Because of this, when the heart contracts it pumps large amounts of blood back into your lungs with each beat. The more this leakage, the more the distension; the more the distension, the more the leakage. We must stop the leakage in order to break this vicious circle."

He then said six words that I will always remember: "I believe we can help you."

Tears came to my eyes when he said those words, and there were tears in his eyes, too. I now knew that I had a chance; I had hope. Dr. Sauvage smiled and squeezed my hand as he turned and left the room. He called Arlene and told her that though the odds were against me surviving the operation, he nonetheless thought I would. He suggested that we pray, and said he was confident God would hear our prayers.

The next morning, November 15, 1989, before the transporter moved me to surgery, Arlene and I prayed together, for we both knew that my surgery was very high-risk. After finishing, we kissed, and then I moved from my bed over onto the gurney and went to the operating room with a feeling of peacefulness that the Lord was with me.

Dr. Sauvage repaired the inlet valve on the left side of my heart so that it no longer leaked, and then he brought me to the intensive care unit, where he supervised my care for the first few hours. When I awakened, Arlene was standing by the bed holding my hand, and I knew that I'd survived. I thanked God and drifted back to sleep.

By the fifth day I was eating well and gaining strength. Dr. Sauvage would drop in to check me over and visit at the oddest hours, usually near midnight but sometimes as late as 3:00

or 4:00 in the morning. Though he stayed only a few minutes on those late visits, we talked just enough about the spiritual side of our lives to make me think long after he had left. The night before I went home, Dr. Sauvage told me that he was cautiously optimistic about my future. After that we talked about the happiness I could find by doing God's work in the rest of my life, however long that might be. He gave me a plastic card bearing the prayer of St. Francis of Assisi, "Lord, Make Me an Instrument of Your Peace," and asked me to read it from time to time. I have done this and found that it helps me maintain a proper perspective of the here and now and of the eternal that lies beyond.

Though I still tired easily when I returned home ten days after my operation, I felt good. Dr. Sauvage would call, often late at night, to check on me and would say with a chuckle, "I knew you'd be home at this hour. How're you doing?" At first I ate well and was gaining strength. But then I started to lose my appetite and the rate of return of my strength slowed down noticeably. In fact, after a few weeks it came to a complete stop, leaving me far below where I wanted to be. Because I'd lost so much weight before surgery and the cold, damp winter weather of Gig Harbor really bothered me, Arlene and I decided to close our home and go south to visit her mother in southern California for a few months of recuperation, believing that the warmer climate there would help me eat better and improve faster. Fortunately, Arlene had a wonderful assistant who could manage the daycare center during the time we planned to be away. This was essential because we now depended on the center's success for our income.

It was late February when we headed south in our motor home, but nothing went right. Each day I became weaker, and two threatening changes occurred. My upper abdomen became enlarged and painful, while my lower legs and feet became swollen and uncomfortable. What appetite I had disappeared. The only good thing was that I wasn't short of breath, but everything else continued to worsen. When we finally reached Arlene's mother's home in Culver City, I was so weak I couldn't walk across the room. We had come south for me to get strong, not to be like this. Our first thought was to see Dr. Taw, who'd taken care of me when we lived in this area years ago. He was current on my case; Dr. Sauvage had sent him copies of my records. When Arlene called for an appointment, his schedule was full but he made room to see me anyway. After a careful examination he said, "Your mitral valve is okay, but you're now in right-heart failure and belong in the hospital." I agreed. Dr. Taw then admitted me to St. John's, where he kept me for seven days and removed 14 pounds of water from my system.

On the morning of my third day in the hospital, Dr. Taw seemed absorbed in deep thought when he came in. He said little while he checked me over and when finished, he sat down in the chair by the side of my bed and said softly, "We must talk." He then spoke with Arlene and me for a long time, and in the kindest way possible told us, "Your heart is worn out, first the left side and now the right. You're tired all the time because the left side can't pump enough blood to nourish your body. Dr. Sauvage repaired the inlet valve on the left side of your heart so it doesn't leak anymore, and this keeps the fluid out of your lungs. But now the right side of your heart has become so distended that its inlet valve can't close when the heart contracts. This causes the heart to pump blood backward into your liver, causing it to distend, and down into your legs, causing them to swell. I'm afraid that you have only a short time to live, perhaps two months, even with the best medical treatment." Arlene and I were stunned. Our bright hopes of but a few weeks before were shattered.

The next day, Dr. Taw asked for consultation from two other cardiologists. After examining me and reviewing my history and laboratory findings, they concurred with his diagnosis and foreboding prediction.

A few days later when I felt somewhat better, Dr. Taw discharged me from the hospital with an appointment for follow-up in his office the next week. Arlene and I had been on an emotional high when we had left Providence in late November, believing that I was going to get better. But now stark reality was at hand: my heart was continuing to give out and had reached the point where it would soon stop. There was no way to improve its function—the muscle structure was worn beyond the possibility of recovery. Despite this devastating information, Arlene and I refused to give up. We wondered if a heart transplant could help me. We called Dr. Taw's office for an earlier appointment. We had to know. The receptionist rearranged his schedule so he could see us the next afternoon. When we saw him, I asked, "Could a transplant help me?"

"Yes, it's your only choice," he said. " I didn't mention it to you before because your age of 64 is beyond the usual cutoff of 60 that most centers adhere to. But if you would like to be considered for a transplant, I'll try to get you accepted for preliminary evaluation at centers that are nearby."

Suddenly, Arlene and I were overwhelmed. Just the thought of having my heart removed and a new one from someone else inserted in its place was too much for either of us to really comprehend without a lot more thought. In fact, at that moment, I didn't even know if I wanted to go that far to try and live longer. Arlene and I needed to go home and face this terrifying determination together. Dr. Taw understood our dilemma. I thanked him for his willingness to help us and said that we would reach him in the morning with our decision.

He said, "That will be fine. In the meantime, if you have any questions, please call me."

We went home and talked and prayed long into the night. While we conversed, I could feel the frequent irregularities of my heart and the waves of weakness that accompanied them. On several occasions during our discussions, these happenings became so severe that they forced me to stop and remain quiet until my heart settled down. These episodes served to highlight my plight and helped us decide to go all out for a new heart.

In the morning I called Dr. Taw and told him what we wanted to do. He was delighted and said he would present my case to his friends at both the well-established UCLA and the newer Cedars Sinai heart transplant clinics in Los Angeles. That afternoon he called us back and said that he had persuaded both clinics to agree to evaluate me.

After preliminary evaluation at both clinics, Arlene and I chose to continue at Cedars because their waiting list was much shorter than UCLA's, with only 11 potential recipients ahead of me instead of 40. This meant I could possibly get a transplant sooner at Cedars, hopefully in time, if I could meet their rigorous criteria and qualify as a candidate to receive a precious donor heart, the vital resource that was in such short supply.

We were both on edge as I began the intense evaluation program at Cedars, which included everything from head to foot—heart, lungs, kidneys, vision and hearing; endocrine, musculoskeletal, brain, neurological and psychological functions; financial situation and family relationships. Our anxiety level was sky high as we waited for the selection board's decision, which would be one of life or death for me. When Debbie Doan, the transplant coordinator, told us two weeks later, "You've been accepted for a heart transplant," I looked upward and said, "Thank You, Jesus."

There are far more patients who need transplants than there are donor hearts available for them. I was one of the fortunate few to be selected. The rest wait to die, usually for only a short time. After Cedars placed my name and transplant requirements in the national registry, Arlene and I began the anxious wait for a suitable donor. The haunting question then became, "Will a donor heart come in time?" I was already approaching the end of the estimated survival time that Dr. Taw had given me.

Debbie gave me a beeper and said, "Wear it all the time except when you're in the shower, and then be no more than six feet away from it." She told us that when it rang, to call Cedars immediately for confirmation that a donor heart was available for me. If it was, I was to come to the hospital within an hour to have my worn-out, old heart replaced by a new, young one. It was a strange and awesome experience to wait and pray for my beeper to go off before it was too late. In essence, I was praying that the family of a brain-dead young accident victim, whose body was being kept alive on a respirator in a hospital somewhere, would consent to having their loved one's healthy, beating heart removed so it could be used to replace mine. This was a deeply emotional experience that I still find hard to describe. I thought about my donor much of the time and wondered who he or she might be and what accident of fate would bring his or her heart to me. I felt a deep sense of reverence for whomever that person might be.

My beeper went off accidentally several times, causing an adrenaline surge throughout my body. Each time this happened my heart nearly stopped. I would reach for the phone, hands shaking with excitement, and clumsily dial the medical center. Life would stand still while Debbie said, "No, Chuck, I'm sorry, it must have been a false alarm." Then with a sense of helplessness, I would put the phone down to wait again.

I carried extra batteries with me and tested my pager frequently to be sure it was working. I was afraid that my chance for a new life would come, and I'd miss it.

Somehow I managed to hang on, though just barely. I was worsening day by day. Then, after two-and-a-half months, a real call came at 5:30 P.M., on August 8, 1990. I called the hospital and was thrilled when Debbie said, "Chuck, come quickly! We've got a heart for you!" I panicked because at that time of day the rush-hour traffic was at its peak and had converted the freeways into gigantic masses of inertia that barely moved. This was my chance for life and there was no way I could get there in time. I told Debbie that the freeways were at near standstill, and I couldn't get to Cedars soon enough. She said, "Go to the Adventist Hospital near you. They have a heliport, and a helicopter will be there to pick you up in 15 minutes." We got there in ten minutes and five minutes later a large Medstar chopper whirled in. A female paramedic opened the door and shouted, "Are you Chuck Medici?"

I said yes, she quickly pulled me in, and away we went.

This was unreal—my mind was a blur. Within 20 minutes, after a $3,000, 40-mile ride, we were at Cedars, and I was soon in the surgery preparation room talking to the anesthesiologist. The procurement team had gone to Long Beach to remove the heart from the donor and wasn't back yet. My old heart was pounding hard and missing beats as I nervously filled out the consent papers. I was both excited and afraid. "Is this really happening?" I thought.

Then the anesthesiologist came back and shocked me with the news that he'd just received a call saying the donor heart wasn't suitable. I was devastated emotionally and physically. The effects of the adrenaline surge that had started when I got the call were now completely gone. I could barely move. I felt lost, as if in a dark and endless crevasse that extended deep into the earth. There was nothing I could do except go home and wait again—mostly likely to die.

When Arlene finally got to the hospital, after what seemed like an eternity, and I sadly told her what had happened, she tried to comfort me by saying half in jest, "This is good practice for the real thing." But it was hard for either of us to smile or even speak. We drove home in silence.

Over a period of days, my courage slowly returned. Arlene was a great help to me in that critical period. Without her support I couldn't have regrouped to continue my race with death. Even though both of us knew that by then my chance of getting a new heart in time was remote, we refused to give up.

Despite the bleakness of my condition, Arlene remained outwardly optimistic and did what had to be done. She sold our home in Gig Harbor and purchased a townhouse for us in Thousand Oaks, a community that was closer to Cedars, so that if I lived to receive a transplant and survived the surgery, we could stay close to the Center to be sure that my body did not reject its new heart. Though we hated to sell the Gig Harbor house, we had to have the money for this transaction. In mid-August we moved from Arlene's mother's home into our new residence.

There were no calls through the rest of August and none in September; my pager was silent, as I continued to worsen.

You never forget "the call," not even for a little while. You look at your beeper and feel for it many times throughout the day and night, and wonder. When?

You live one day at a time when you're waiting for a donor heart. You can't count on tomorrow. By late September, I was so weak I knew the end was near and had all but given up hope that a heart would come in time for me.

Then it happened! My beeper alarmed at 7:30 P.M. on October 10, 1990. Barely able to hold the phone, I dialed the center. Then I heard the words we had been praying to hear as Debbie said, "Chuck, come quickly! We've got another heart for you!" My eyes so filled with tears and my throat so choked that I could barely see and scarcely speak. But somehow I said, "Thank God! We're coming!"

Our heads were awhirl—this was it! Arlene drove me to the center as fast as possible, arriving in good time as we were now closer and traffic on the freeway had thinned out by that time. They were ready for me when I came through the door. This was for real, and things happened fast. I was sedated, shaved from chin to knees, and readied for surgery. Arlene and I prayed together, after which I told her, "I'll see you later, kiddo." Then, in a dreamy, half-awake state, with a feeling of part fear and part peace, I was wheeled off to the surgery and placed on the operating table in the transplant room, where I would wait for my new heart to arrive from afar.

Dr. Alfredo Trento and his procurement team had flown to San Francisco in a corporate jet to remove the heart from a 19-year-old brain-dead accident victim. The implant team at Cedars would await word from them that they were within an hour of bringing the heart into the surgery before Dr. Arnold Friedman, my anesthesiologist, would put me to sleep and Dr. Carlos Blanche, my surgeon, and his team would open my chest and expose the heart. But they'd wait to place me on the heart-lung machine until my new heart was actually in the operating room, to shorten my time on the "pump." As soon as it was there, they'd quickly put me on the machine, remove my old heart, and suture the new one in its place. Timing would be critical to the success of this elaborate procedure, which required frequent communication and precise coordination between the two teams that at one point would be 350 miles apart.

While the Cedars team awaited for the word to start, I lay on the operating table asking myself: "Do I really want to do this?" I did. The lights were dimmed, and Dr. Friedman played soft, soothing music to help me relax, but waiting in that operating room for my new heart to come from far away was an unreal experience. I was emotionally overwhelmed, started to doze lightly, and prayed, in my semiconscious state, for God to help me get through this.

In those twilight moments my life passed before me. I could see my mother and father and my brother in my youth. I could see Arlene as she was when I first saw her at GTE in my early days there—beautiful, flowing red hair, cameo features and lovely smile. I could see her sweet face the day I asked her to marry me.

Then the call came—they were approaching L.A.! The Cedars team swung into action. Dr. Friedman began my anesthetic and I drifted off to sleep. Dr. Blanche opened my chest and when all was ready, placed me on the heart-lung machine, removed my sick, old heart, and replaced it with my donor's heart, which was healthy, strong and 45 years younger. During the surgery I could hear people talking in the background and could even feel the vibration of my breastbone as it was being sawed apart. Though I felt no real pain, I knew what was happening and wanted more anesthesia. But I couldn't move even a finger to signal anyone. A few days later I asked Dr. Friedman if I could've heard voices and felt the surgery. He said, "Yes, it's possible, because your condition was so bad that I couldn't give you more anesthetic without endangering your life."

I made a remarkable recovery. By the third day I was walking easily and could feel the power of my new heart. This was so different than I'd been with my old heart just three days before, barely able to walk 50 feet.

I was discharged from the hospital 14 days after my transplant, feeling good physically and energized mentally by the realization that a whole new life was in front of me. I continued to make good progress after going to our townhouse, where Arlene fed me all I could eat. Everything tasted good. I gained strength and put on real weight. Soon I had the energy to do anything I wanted. I looked younger and felt better than I had in years. It seemed like a miracle. It was!

But my troubles were not over yet because after a few weeks, my body began to reject its new heart. Arlene was very wise in having bought our townhouse, as I needed to stay close to Cedars until this emerging threat could be defeated. During that critical period, the staff treated this reaction by adjusting the dosage of the powerful medications they gave to block my immune system's attacks on my new heart. To guide the administration of these medicines, Dr. Lawrence Czer, the transplant cardiologist at Cedars, took tiny pieces of tissue, called biopsies, from the inside of my transplanted heart and examined them under the microscope to determine how much I needed. When he found that the rejection reaction was prominent, he increased the dosage of the drugs, and when he found that the reaction was subsiding, he decreased the dosage.

Dr. Czer has thus far done this biopsy procedure 24 times in the five-and-a-half years since my operation. He obtains these biopsies by passing a long, slender, flexible instrument with a grasping tip through a vein in the right side of my neck. He guides the end of this special forceps down into the main pumping chamber of the right side of my heart, where he engages the wall and snips off a small piece. Dr. Czer does this procedure while I'm awake, using only local anesthesia in the area where he inserts the instrument. At first I was apprehensive when he did this, but after the first few times I got over my fear. My biopsy schedule was weekly for the first month, then every two weeks for three months, then monthly for nine months, then every six months for a year, and now yearly for the past three years. Needless to say, we were delighted when Debbie, a real professional, with whom we had become good friends, told me after I'd completed the monthly biopsy schedule, "Everything is fine now. You may go home!"

After that welcome release, we closed our Thousand Oaks townhouse and put it up for sale. As soon as the arrangements were in order, we headed north to Gig Harbor in our motor home on February 6, 1992. This was the day for which we'd prayed. An amazing, almost unbelievable period in our lives had now come to a close. In the two years since we'd left Gig Harbor to go south for me to recuperate from surgery, I'd been given a new life and was going home with another person's heart in my chest. While we were now broke financially, we were rich in all the ways that really counted. I was healthy again, and we had each other. Since my transplant, I have thanked God every day for my new life.

We made good time and reached Gig Harbor in three days. When we pulled up and parked to the side of Arlene's daycare center, we knew that at last we were really home. We decided to stay right there and set up housekeeping in our 272-square-foot motor home, for this was all we had. Years ago we would have been unhappy with such cramped conditions and meager finances. But what we had lived through had set our priorities straight. We both knew we had all that really mattered.

After two years of living in our motor home, we rented a house and have enjoyed the increased space and many conveniences that this has given us. But of far greater importance, we've come to appreciate even more as the years have passed that the true joy of life is the happiness we experience, and that this comes from our attitude and what we do, and not from things. It is a matter of people, of children, of love, of caring, of sharing and of God. Arlene has a plaque on the wall of our home that says this in a different but beautiful way: "Home is where the heart is."

People say to me, "You were really brave to have gone through all that high-risk heart surgery." While that may be correct, I answer that the really brave one was Arlene, who went through the agony and the endless hours of waiting and praying for me to survive.

I've been asked, "Would you go through it again?" Life has become so precious that, if my new heart were rejected, I'd gladly do it again if another donor were available to me. The inclusive cost of my heart transplant, including all the biopsies, is now approximately $300,000. I thank God for my GTE insurance coverage, which has enabled me to have this life-renewing surgery and follow-up care. Even more, I thank God for my donor and his family, who gave me the gift of continued life. Without my donor's heart, I would have died years ago.

I often think about having someone else's heart in my chest, pumping the blood throughout my body upon which my life depends. This is a very emotional thought for me. For the first year I never really felt that it was *my* heart. I considered that it belonged to my 19-year-old donor, whom I named "Bill." But since then I have been able to think of his heart as part mine, too. Bill also helps me realize how dependent we all are on one another.

I don't know whether this makes any sense, but before my surgery I couldn't stand to listen to the music of the popular rock singer Elton John. Now, since my transplant, I love his music and play his tapes frequently. I wonder if "Bill" has changed me.

I tried many times during the first year to write a letter of thanks to my donor's family, but each time I became so emotional, I couldn't finish it. How do you thank someone for giving you life at the expense of their loved one? Finally, after the first year, I was able to complete the letter and send it to the national donor registry, where it was forwarded to the family. (Neither the donor's family nor the recipient are ever told the other's identity.) The key sentence in that letter to "Bill's" parents is: "My wife and I thank you from the bottom of our spiritual hearts for the life-giving gift of your son's physical heart, which enables me to live."

I don't fear death anymore because I know that the next life can be an infinitely greater experience. And when God calls me to eternity, I hope I'll be ready to go. In the meantime, I'm here to do His work and be happy. One of my goals now is to develop a program to encourage people to sign up to be organ donors so that others like me may live.

When I reflect back on my earlier years and realize I didn't have the happiness then that I do now, I'm deeply thankful for the progress I've made in my spiritual journey. I've learned to live this life one day at a time. I've learned to be happy today.

I no longer wait to tell Arlene I love her. And she doesn't wait to tell me. Today is what we have. *This* day.

Comments by Dr. Sauvage

Though my partners and I performed about 800 open-heart operations a year at the Providence Medical Center in Seattle, we did not do transplants because the scarcity of donor hearts restricted that type of care in western Washington to the University of Washington Teaching Hospital.

Of the several thousand patients for whom I performed open-heart surgery during my career, only two have thus far had to subsequently undergo a heart transplant, and Chuck was the first. Both patients had their transplants at Cedars Sinai in Los Angeles and both have done well. Each was beyond the cut-off age for most other centers, being 64 and 66 years respectively at the time of their transplants.

I did not fully appreciate the magnitude of the emotional stress that many of the patients who receive heart transplants undergo until Mary Ann and I went to Gig Harbor and interviewed Chuck and Arlene in their mobile home, alongside the daycare center. When Chuck had reached the point where a transplant was his only chance, he and Arlene chose life over death. Many patients on waiting lists die before a donor heart becomes available for them, and Chuck was near the end when his came. I shudder when I think of what it must have been like to be helicoptered to Cedars and then told that the donor's heart in Long Beach wasn't suitable.

Heart transplantation is no longer an experimental procedure. It is now a proven treatment for patients like Chuck whose hearts have lost so much of their ability to contract that they can't sustain life for long, even at a low level of function. Today, five-and-a-half years after his transplant, Chuck looks the picture of health and feels good because of "Bill's" heart in his chest. Unfortunately, there are far more patients who need transplants than there are donor hearts. Last year only about 2,500 heart transplants could be performed in the United States because there were no more donor hearts. Since the need is far greater, when I renewed my drivers license three years ago, I gave permission to remove my organs for transplantation to benefit others should I be involved in an accident that would render me brain-dead. I would appreciate if all who read these words would consider doing the same. Chuck is living proof of the value of someone somewhere having done this. Because of that gift Chuck is alive today, and he and Arlene are proving that love is what life is all about.

It's Wonderful to Be Like New Again

Merilyn Sanders

It's hard to see your parents age and watch their bodies wear out. I live in a basement apartment off the back porch of my parents' home, so I can help my dad who's 89. What I'm doing now is my way of paying him back for all he's done for me. Mom died two years ago of a virulent cancer when she was 88. Losing her after 68 years was very hard on Dad, who is deaf and nearly blind. Mom took care of him until a few weeks before she died.

Dad has another problem. He lost his right arm when he was 16; a shotgun blast at close range blew it off above the elbow. But that didn't stop him. He became a plastering contractor and worked all his life, holding the hod under the stump of his right arm and slapping the plaster on with his good left arm.

My folks did the best they could for us kids, despite having little to their name. I was born at home in South Beloit, Illinois, on December 17, 1935, during the Great Depression, the fourth child of seven. Dad worked where and when he could at his trade, and Mom worked in the shoe factory. Somehow, though, one of them always seemed to be with us. Though there wasn't much else, there was always lots of love in our home. In addition, Mom and Dad instilled a deep love of God in us, too, even though they didn't take us to a special church.

When I was 13 we moved to Yakima, the agricultural center in the middle of Washington state, because Dad thought he could get more work there. He did, but it was still hard for him with only one arm. Going from a six-room schoolhouse in Beloit to a junior high school in Yakima, where there were six rooms for each grade, was a difficult transition for me. I muddled through my classes and dropped out when I was 17 to marry John, who was 19. He didn't finish school, either. For the first couple of years we lived in the attic of his folks' home. There was neither heat nor water up there, and we had to be careful not to hit our heads on the two-by-fours that were close above. The only good thing about that attic was the roof—it didn't leak. During the winter our space was cold as ice, and we had to cuddle up under all the covers we could find to keep warm.

John's folks didn't have much, and we both did any kind of work we could, from picking fruit to cleaning up, just to eat. Finally, after two years, John landed a steady job as a maintenance man for the Yakima Valley Transportation Line, a branch of the Union Pacific Railroad, that hauled fruit to the warehouses for storage, and later took it from there to the main railroad for shipment to the big cities in the East. His work was hard and often dangerous. In 1960 he severely injured his back on the job. Despite two operations to ease the pain, he could never work again. The Union Pacific finally gave him a small pension, but from the time of his injury I had to support him and our children—Debbie, who was born in 1957, John Jr., born in 1961, and Brenda, born in 1963.

After working at fill-in positions here and there as best I could, I finally got a steady job in 1964 as a waitress at a new Chinese restaurant in Yakima called the Dragon Inn, and worked there until 1991. A lot happened in those 27 years. I went from waiting tables to being the head waitress, with the responsibility for all the hiring and firing. And then, toward the end, to being only a part-time worker. My shift started at 4:00 in the afternoon and continued until we closed, sometime between midnight and 2:00 in the morning. In my biggest year at the Dragon I made almost $8,000, counting tips, of course. John looked after the children while I worked. He did the best he could, but he always felt he should be working instead of me. He couldn't adapt to being a househusband, and this gradually got to him. He became depressed, hard to get along with, and then took to the bottle. As time passed, I did, too.

Our two younger children, John Jr. and Brenda, became addicted to drugs while they were teenagers. It was hard for me to keep rein on them while they were growing up because I was away, working from the late afternoon to the early-morning hours.

Somehow, by the grace of God, John Jr. was eventually able to kick his habit and later married Tina, a great girl, who has been a devoted wife to him. They have three children, a boy and two girls, and Grandma couldn't be happier about that.

Tragically, Brenda's story is much different. She couldn't stop drugs, continued to lose control of her life, and was eventually killed by her addiction, being found dead in Astoria, Oregon three years ago. The police said she died of an overdose. During the last two years of her life I heard nothing from her and didn't even know where she was. It's terrible to have a child of yours go that way. I think of her every day.

The stresses of my life in the late 1970s became too much for me. I became confused, couldn't cope anymore, and began to see things that weren't there as my world came crashing down around me. I completely lost it and had to be committed to a mental ward for six weeks. After that I was at home, under the care of a psychiatrist for six months more.

When my mind began to clear, I started the long process of rebuilding my life. The first step was to commit to stop drinking, and the second was to begin the search for greater meaning in my life. At first I craved a drink and could hardly resist the temptation. But little by little I overcame that weakness. Regaining my self-confidence took even longer, nearly a year. Finally, after that long period, I was able to return to work at the Dragon.

During that period, Debbie, our oldest, helped me get my life in order by encouraging me to trust in God and to believe in myself. She had left home before her brother and sister got into trouble with drugs and married Don Franklin, whom John and I liked from the first time we met him. Shortly after their marriage, they became interested in the Jehovah's Witness religion, and a year later they embraced that faith. Both found great happiness in their new beliefs. Debbie, imbued with a missionary zeal, was determined that I would come to believe as she did. We had many discussions about her convictions that planted seeds of interest in my mind. She didn't miss a chance to enlighten me and left the Jehovah's magazine, *Watchtower,* around the house whenever she visited us. Before long I started reading it, and even John would occasionally turn a page or two.

John tried to reform his life, too. After I returned to work he attempted to stay dry, but he occasionally lost control and fell off the wagon. One of those times was the night he had his first heart attack in 1985. He had gone out while I was working late at the Dragon and had staggered back just in time to get in bed before I got home. He didn't want me to know, but I could easily tell from his slurred speech that he'd taken far too much. I was upset, told him so, got in bed, turned over and went to sleep. When he woke me about an hour later, I said, "Be quiet and let me sleep." About a half hour later he woke me again. This time he was having trouble breathing. I turned the light on and could see that he was not only gasping for breath, but his face was ashen and his eyes were filled with terror. He put a hand out to me and struggled to say, "Help!" He looked like death was near. Instantly I became terrified, too, and said, "Oh my God," as I jumped up and dialed 911. The medics came quickly and took him to the hospital, where the heart specialist said John was having a massive heart attack and would die that night. But he rallied and was able to leave the hospital after several weeks. Over the next three years John had three more heart attacks and remained an invalid throughout. His days were difficult. Finally, after a massive stroke, he died at home on June 13, 1988.

Though both John and I had our faults, we loved each other dearly. I wish that his life could have been easier, but despite all his pain and disability, he seldom complained. In his last months he seemed at peace with himself and all of us, as if he were preparing to die. I believe that had he lived a few months more, he would have become a Jehovah's Witness.

Because of Debbie, I had developed an increasing interest in the Jehovah's Witness faith, and during John's lingering illness, I began to read their Bible in earnest. Without question, my emerging faith in Jehovah helped me survive the long ordeal of John's dying, by giving me the spiritual strength to prevent the disruptive stresses of my life during that somber time from taking me down again.

Six months after John's death, I dedicated my life to Jehovah and was baptized a Witness on December 17, 1988. I accepted all Jehovah's teachings and commands, including that I had to be willing to die rather than receive blood because if I did, I would be damned forever. I understood that if I were ever to need surgery, it would be my responsibility to find a surgeon who would promise to let me die rather than give blood to save my life.

The teachings about blood had special meaning to me because every doctor who had ever listened to my chest, even as a child, had heard a heart murmur. They had made light of it until I had a little stroke several months after John had his first heart attack. When that happened, I lost my memory and had trouble speaking for a few days. Fortunately, I then recovered quickly and returned to work at the Dragon ten days later. Dr. Preacher, a heart specialist, followed me carefully after that. He said that my trouble had been caused by a tiny clot that had broken loose from my heart valve and been carried by the blood into the vessels of my brain, where it caused the stroke. Dr. Preacher told me I had been born with an abnormal valve at the main outlet of my heart. He said this valve had only two cusps instead of the normal three, and that valves with two cusps don't work right and tend to get small clots on them. Over time they also become thick and stiff and block the passage of blood. But he said my valve still moved well enough that I could go back to work.

I went back to waiting tables and did fine for the next six years, but my success was deceptive. A year before I had my stroke, the Dragon's business had begun to fall off, and over the ensuing years the owner had to cut my hours back more and more. It got so bad that by late 1990, I could barely support myself on the little I made. At that point I had to look elsewhere for work. But for many months I could find nothing better. Then in the summer of 1991, my luck changed when I applied for a job at the Golden Wheel, a nearby Chinese restaurant, and was hired the next day. This restaurant had become the Dragon's main competitor and had taken most of its clientele.

Unlike the Dragon, the Golden Wheel had lots of customers, and I noticed right away that I had trouble doing what the boss expected me to do because after a few hours I would become exhausted and develop trouble breathing. I couldn't get enough air. This scared me so much that I frequently prayed to Jehovah, asking Him to make me stronger. Instead I got weaker. Worst of all, I nearly blacked out three times while carrying big trays of Chinese food. The first two times I was lucky. I was able to grasp the side of an empty booth for support and collapse on the seat in a heap, just as I was about to faint. Somehow nothing spilled when I dropped those two trays on the table, and no one saw me go down. Both times I sat there until my head cleared, and when I was okay, I got up and continued working. The third time it happened, I wasn't so fortunate. There was no place to sit. Everything went dark, and I fell to the floor with a crash. It was a real mess, fried rice and all the rest from here to there, with me sprawled out in the middle of it. This time I couldn't hide what had happened, and when I got my senses back, the boss sent me home and told me not to come back until my doctor gave the okay.

I went to Dr. Preacher and told him what had happened. He said, "Merilyn, this is serious. It's what I was afraid might happen. We must do special studies right away to find what has to be done." Then after the echocardiogram and heart catheterization were completed, he said, "The main outlet valve from your heart is closing off, and this is causing your heart to fail. You must have open-heart surgery very soon."

With those words, the full impact of my commitment to never receive a blood transfusion came crashing down on me. Jehovah was testing me. I was scared but knew what I had to do. I told Dr. Preacher, "I want the operation, but I'm a Jehovah's Witness and would rather die than receive blood." He said he understood and would send me to Dr. Sauvage at the Providence Medical Center in Seattle because he took care of many Jehovah's Witness patients without using any blood. The liaison committee from my church agreed. Dr. Sauvage came well recommended.

Nonetheless, I was frightened and wondered if I would bleed to death. I cried on and off for several days. While I desperately wanted to live, I could not agree under any circumstances to the use of blood, even if it meant losing my life. I prayed to Jehovah for help, and He gave me courage. No question I was still fearful, but that was not going to stop me from moving ahead to regain my health.

I knew that there was no time to procrastinate, for I was worsening rapidly. Just climbing up the stairs from my basement apartment had become very difficult for me. In fact, it had become nearly impossible. When I finally did get to that top step, I would be so short of breath and weak that I could not talk and had to lean against the wall to keep from falling. I would have to stay that way until my breathing improved and my legs lost their rubbery feeling. Sometimes this would take 10 minutes.

Debbie came to help and took me to Seattle to see Dr. Sauvage. I was apprehensive when we opened the door to his office and walked in. But when he walked into the room where his staff had placed me, I could sense an air of confidence about him that made me feel better. Still my worry was: would he promise to do my operation without giving me any blood, even if that meant I would die? If he wouldn't, I'd have to find a different heart surgeon who would make that pledge to me.

Dr. Sauvage asked me many questions about my condition and my previous state of health. He then examined me and studied the X rays that Dr. Preacher had taken. When he was finished, he said he agreed that I needed a new aortic valve. At that point I told him I was a Jehovah's Witness and couldn't receive blood. He said, "I know, Dr. Preacher told me. I don't want you to worry. I'm confident you'll do well, and I promise that I will never give you blood under any circumstances." He then went on to say that he admired my unwavering commitment to my beliefs, even though he was not of my faith. He told me I had more to do in this life, and that it was a privilege for him to help me so I could serve Jehovah in the years ahead. That did it for me. I knew he understood how important my religion was to me, and I wanted to hug him on the spot.

I went into the hospital feeling secure and was prepared for surgery. Nonetheless, that night before my operation was a long one. Toward midnight Dr. Sauvage stopped in and checked me over. As he turned to leave, he said, "I'm confident God will bless our work for you." This made me feel better, and I dozed off. When I awoke, I went to surgery with a sense of peace.

My operation went well. Dr. Sauvage was very careful, and I lost only half a pint of blood. My aortic valve was like rock, with only a tiny opening off to one side through which blood could barely pass. He removed my old valve and implanted an artificial one in its place that worked like new.

When the operation was over, I woke up quickly and was taken to the intensive care unit where Dr. Sauvage brought Mom in to see me. When she started to cry, he put his arm around her shoulder and said, "Dear, the danger is past. Merilyn is fine." Mom often spoke about how those few words calmed her fears.

I had no problems and went home six days later. The night before I left, Dr. Sauvage and I talked at length about the rest of my life. He told me my heart was excellent, and that I could look forward to a long and active life. This made me very happy.

I regained my strength quickly and returned to work at the Golden Wheel five weeks later. It's now just over four years since my surgery, and I'm still working a full shift without getting tired. I can even run up the stairs from my apartment without getting short of breath. It's wonderful to be like new again.

As remarkable as my physical recovery has been, my spiritual advancement is even more amazing. As I look back over my life, I now see my nervous breakdown and my heart trouble as blessings in disguise that have helped me to focus my life and better appreciate each day. In that same sense I have also come to realize that my prayers are always answered, though the answer may not always be what I had asked for. I accept what Jehovah decides is best for me.

Had I not had my nervous breakdown, there's no telling where I might be today because I was going in the wrong direction when I began to come apart. That experience turned me around and steered me toward Jehovah so He could heal my soul.

The spiritual events that I experienced with my heart disease have moved me to a new level of appreciation of who I am and where I'm going. I now see each day more clearly as a gift from Jehovah and as a joy in itself. I find happiness by looking after my dad and by trying to help everyone I know and everyone I serve at the Golden Wheel. I'm doing Jehovah's work in this world, and I'm happier than I've ever been.

Comments by Dr. Sauvage

I developed a considerable reputation in the Jehovah's Witness community as a result of performing many successful open-heart operations for their members without the use of blood. In fact, I liked the challenge of doing heart surgery that way.

If a surgeon agrees to do surgery for a Witness, he or she must solemnly promise not to give blood, even to save the patient's life. I made such a promise to Merilyn and felt comfortable that she would do well, even though the margin of safety that the ability to transfuse her could provide wouldn't be available. Despite absence of this safety factor, the great majority of Jehovah's Witness patients go through open-heart surgery without any trouble and convalesce rapidly. I believe that their courage and will to live have a lot to do with their rapid recovery.

Though I don't agree with the Jehovah's Witnesses' interpretation of the Bible as it pertains to blood transfusions and certain other issues, I deeply respect these people. In fact, in this modern era when many lack firm belief in anything spiritual, it was a privilege for me to take care of patients who would bravely have given their lives for what they believed.

Though Merilyn was fearful, she went ahead and had the operation she needed. She didn't question her faith. She accepted it and found strength in her beliefs.

Now that there is increasing concern about contracting disease from transfusion of blood for fear that it could be infected by viruses, many patients who are *not* of the Jehovah's Witness faith are requesting that their surgeons *avoid* giving them any blood unless it is absolutely necessary. I believe that they are correct in doing this and, if a member of my family or I were to require open-heart surgery, I would make such a request, too!

Though all of my patients are special to me, Merilyn occupies a unique place in my heart because she was my *last* patient. Mary Ann and I had decided after much prayerful thought that I would retire from clinical surgery on December 1, 1991, two weeks after I had reached my 65th birthday. After a very busy last year in which I did perhaps my best work, Merilyn was to be my last case, with her operation scheduled for Saturday, November 30. When I walked into the surgery that morning it was hard for me to appreciate that this day had really come, after 33 nonstop years. In some sense it seemed like all the rest. As I washed at the scrub sink for the last time before entering the operating room to gown and glove, I prayed as I always did for the skill to do as good an operation for my patient as I had ever done for anyone. I believe God heard my prayers and guided my hands during Merilyn's surgery.

After Merilyn's heart was pumping again and working well with its new valve in place, I began to close her chest. Right then a powerful surge of emotion overwhelmed me. At that moment, after thousands of cases, I fully realized that she was *really* the last. My days in the operating room would soon be over. Within seconds my eyes so filled with tears that I could barely see the wound. I had to stop. I was emotionally drained, but after a minute or two I was able to partially

regain my composure and continue. As I completed the closure of Merilyn's wound, I said a silent prayer thanking God
for enabling me to end my clinical career by doing an excellent operation for her.

The next several weeks were very difficult for me as I
slowly adjusted to my life after surgery. I want to emphasize
that I was not sad or depressed, and yet during those weeks I
would be seized for no apparent reason with sudden episodes
of tears and inability to speak that would last for a few minutes, several times a day, while I was working at the research
institute. When I went home in the evening, I would ask Mary
Ann if she thought I was losing my marbles. She told me that
I needed patience. She was right. After six weeks I was okay.
Those strange episodes stopped.

For these past four years I have directed the extensive
research programs of The Hope Heart Institute as a full-time
volunteer, and have enjoyed every moment of doing so. While
I loved my days in clinical surgery, I cherish what I do now,
too, because there is so much good that we can do for so many
through research. Each experiment is an exciting adventure in
learning that has the potential to help millions of people the
world over.

A special joy of my new schedule is that now I get home
every evening at a reasonable hour for dinner with Mary Ann,
and I am with her and our children and grandchildren much
more than ever before. During our August vacation on the
shores of the straits of Juan de Fuca, the children and their
families join us at our retreat for days that are filled with happiness. In addition, in my current relaxed life, Mary Ann and
I do many things that we couldn't before. We'll often just pick
up and go out for dinner and a movie, ball game or concert.
We also take a long walk nearly every evening and tell each

other about our respective days and talk about all kinds of things. This is indeed a special period in our lives.

My retirement from surgery has also given me the quiet time that I have needed to write this book. This experience has been a wonderful occasion for my own personal reflection and spiritual advancement. In this process I have come to more deeply appreciate St. Francis's beautiful prayer as an exceedingly important guide for all of us in attaining the happiness we seek in this life and the next.

Following the
Spirit Within

Lester Sauvage, M.D.

Through our lives and our faith, my patients and I have affirmed the validity of the three-part spiritual action plan that I presented at the beginning of this book, and that has helped us experience greater joy in our lives:

1. Embrace each day to the fullest.
2. Talk to God and listen, too.
3. Serve God by serving humanity.

This three-step plan, which is directed primarily to the spirit, also has a supportive and an invigorating influence on the functions of the physical body. This effect on our bodies is mediated through the positive mind-body relationships that this plan engenders as a result of the increased flow of happiness it promotes in our lives. My patients and I now ask you to follow the Spirit of God within your soul and reexamine this plan to see if it could be of aid in your life, too.

1. Embrace Each Day to the Fullest

Patsy, after four open-heart surgeries, tells us not to wait to say what's in our hearts. She wisely tells us to do it today while we still have time. She asks us to tell our wife or husband, our children, our grandchildren, our parents and our friends that we love them. We can't go back and do it yesterday. We can't go forward and do it tomorrow. We can only do it today. The ever-present *now* is the only time we have, and this very moment is a cause for joy. Let's not delay—tomorrow may never come, and yesterday, for sure, is gone. This very day could be my last. If that should prove to be the case, what would I want to do today? This thought makes me pause and ponder. Yes, what if? One thing is certain—to answer this formidable question I must decide what's most important in my life. As Joe said, God and family are most important. I hope that I would thank God for having given me another day, do my work to the best of my ability, be kind to all whom I would meet, tell my precious wife that I love her with all my heart and soul, and say something supportive to each of our children and grandchildren. In considering the agenda for our last day, we can all learn from Anna, who at 92 knows that her time is short, but gratefully accepts each day as a precious gift from God in which she finds happiness, despite her age and infirmities. Anna quietly lives today as if it were her last and doesn't make a fuss about it. She has her priorities right, and knows that she is maintained in existence from nothing to something by the sustaining power of God. In this light, Anna, with great wisdom, sees our world and herself in the accurate context of reality.

It isn't easy for any of us to admit that we are frail and must one day die. But once we do and accept the realities of our earthly journey, we are liberated from the fear of this transition and are able to more fully embrace each day. My faith, my family, my patients and my research have helped me envision life as a ride on a passenger train to eternity. The length of the track over which each of our trains must pass varies in a manner that is analogous to the maximum duration of our finite earthly lives and is determined by the genetic code in our cells, a biologic determinant that is unique to each of us. Doctors can't extend this distance. But they can often help us stay on our metaphorical speeding train for a longer time and get us closer to the end of the line, perhaps even to reach it. Nonetheless, despite the best of medical care, few of us will travel that far. Instead, our ride will usually be terminated prematurely by disease or injury, which stops our train and takes us off into eternity at that point. But if this does not happen, we will ride to the end of the line where it will be "all out" at the terminal station of advanced old age. There will be no return trip to earthly life, only on to our eternal destiny, which can be a time of infinite happiness if we have led our lives in a manner pleasing to God.

My progress down the track of my own life has been an eventful journey, the mental vision of which now enables me to acknowledge and accept without sadness or fear that I passed its midpoint some time ago. How far back is not important. To paraphrase Mother Teresa, what matters is the good I can do this day and the love with which I do it. And if my actions are driven by love, God will reward me with His gifts of peace and joy, which are essential to my spiritual life. Each day can bring me great happiness if I follow the Spirit within my soul and accept God's invitation to be my brothers' and my sisters' keeper.

When we endeavor to make each day part of a dynamic journey to a greater destiny, in which we serve God by serving humanity with love out of our open hearts, we find high purpose in all we do and gain a sense of our majestic human worth. Through this process we are blessed to experience the fullness of human happiness. This is true regardless of our job, be it digging a ditch, serving as a doctor or nurse, driving a truck, running a major corporation, working in a factory or on a farm, ministering as a priest or nun, or raising a family. Empowered by this grace and wisdom, we can reach out and embrace today to the fullest, while at the same time being thankful for the yesterday that was and for the tomorrow that is yet to come.

2. Talk to God and Listen, Too

It's no accident that I found few atheists on the operating table because our spirits cry out for help when we are threatened. Fortunately, as Marta in her youth and Anna in her age tell us, we are not alone. God is near. He is within. He is love, and love is a mystery. He doesn't leave us, even when we forget Him or doubt that He exists.

Through their close encounters with physical death as a consequence of heart disease and surgery, my patients learned to talk to the God within their souls and to listen to Him. From those conversations they gained confidence, peace, joy and a great determination to get better.

We all need to turn within and talk to God, whatever our personal interpretation of divinity may be. We need this quiet time between our inner selves and the Holy Spirit. We need it every day, when we are just one-on-one with God. This is what prayer is all about, whether formal or informal. We don't need to be in church to talk with God, although it often helps. I find that stopping in the chapel for brief visits recharges my spiritual batteries and helps me get these conversations started. I need to talk with God frequently to keep my spiritual life in balance and progressing in the right direction. I often prayed in surgery and asked for help. When the going was critical, and one stitch to control a bleeding vessel far behind the heart could make the difference between life and death, my prayer was simple: "Not my skill, Lord, but Thine." Somehow the stitch was always right; the bleeding stopped. Some may say it was self-hypnosis; I believe it was something else—that God heard my prayers and guided my hands.

Joe, June, Billy and all the rest of my patients whom you have met have come to see life itself as a form of prayer. Each has found that God is their best friend. None of us needs a special connection or credit card to talk to Him. God is waiting for us on the other end of a toll-free line. My patients in so many ways are urging you and me to make that call!

A conversation with God involves talking and listening— just as when we converse with one another. You and I talk first and He listens—that part is easy. God talks second and we listen—that part is hard. First, we must stop talking before we can listen. Second, we must be attentive in order to hear His words. They may come to me as a soft voice from within that brings a sense of peace, or they may come in the form of a question, comment or suggestion from my wife, former patients, co-workers in the research institute, my parish priest, friends, or even strangers. His words may also come from one of our children, daughters-in-law, sons-in-law, or in the smile of a grandchild who wants a hug. In fact, His words may come to me from any source whatsoever.

God's words may come to you in similar or different ways, but they will come just as surely. God may also speak to you and me through the tranquility of a walk along a mountain trail, the progressive radiance of the rising sun, the splendor of the setting sun with its red afterglow, the power of the ocean, or the peace and stillness of the night with the vast universe extending above into the endless realms of distant space. Yes, by these means and so many more, God speaks to us and guides our course toward happiness by encouraging us to serve those in need.

3. Serve God by Serving Humanity

We find joy by serving others. This key to what we all want and need is so self-evident that I'm afraid we may tend to miss the obvious. God doesn't hide His answer to the question that is foremost in our lives: "How may I find increased happiness in my life?" To the contrary, He answers loud and clear and places His response directly before us. Let's open our hearts and follow His instructions that flow from the Ten Commandments and the Beatitudes, such as "Love Thy Neighbor as Thy Self" and the Golden Rule. When we do this, God rewards us with His priceless gifts of peace and joy. The wonderful truth is that serving God in this way is so easy if we don't let pride, arrogance and selfishness get in our way. Following the Spirit within our souls brings joy into our lives. Mac found happiness by running his business to provide a living for his 200 employees and their families. Merilyn finds happiness by looking after her dad, who at 89 would otherwise have to be in a nursing home, and by serving her customers at the restaurant. Joe finds happiness by taking care of his family and by helping homeless people.

Doing good for others out of love always brings us happiness, and the opportunity to do this is ever close at hand for all of us. It is as near as the next individual with whom we come in contact. We can start this process by being pleasant to that person. But we can't attain this priceless mental state if our spiritual hearts are closed. Let's open them wide so that goodness can flow out to those around us and happiness can flow in as a result of our actions. The Holy Spirit of God within our souls waits for us to do this. All that is required for you and me to be happy is to follow wherever He may lead us.

You may recall I said earlier that I asked my patients before their surgeries what happiness was to them, and most found this question difficult to answer. After a few minutes of discussion about this all-important aspect of our lives, I gave them my definition: *"Happiness is that peace of mind, serenity of soul,and exhilaration of spirit that God gives us when we, out of love, serve those who need us."* I asked my patients to use the quiet periods that illness and surgery provided to probe their souls and plot their courses toward increased happiness in the extended years that their operations would bring them. I suggested that they could do this best by allowing God to open their spiritual hearts still wider and by accepting His invitation to make the helping of others an even higher priority in their lives. My patients who have told you their stories did this and experienced increased happiness, whether they were rich or poor or somewhere in between. From youth to old age, from housewife to widow, from waitress to venture capitalist, from plumber to service manager, and from mechanic to company president, they are now finding great joy by living their lives out of love, out of their open hearts.

As Billy says, "When I've done my best, I'm happy, whether I finish first, middle or dead last." We are successful in God's eyes when we've done all we could. We must accept the limits of what we can do, but not less. That's all God asks. He simply requests that we do our best and leave the rest to Him.

We can make the world a better place for everyone by developing our own unique talents to the fullest, becoming the best person we can be, and sharing ourselves and what we have with others out of love. Fortunately, this is also the surest way to become the happiest person we can be. This is a formula that never fails because it is part of our unchanging human nature. Happiness, in reality, is our destiny—if we don't fight it. My patients are saying that it's never too late for any of us to change our course, become the Good Samaritans of today, and find the happiness we seek.

If each of us, in the rest of our lives, could inspire even two or three people to follow our example and find increased happiness by helping others, and they in turn could do the same, etc., etc., etc., the ripple effect of our combined actions would become a mighty force for good that could not be stopped. Together we could make the world a better place for all in one generation. Let's do it!

Closing Comment: The Inspiration of St. Francis of Assisi

During the past 21 years, St. Francis has become an increasingly important part of my life. When the whole family visited Assisi in Italy on our first international family excursion back in 1975, I had only a superficial appreciation of him. Then I was more interested in the pigeons around the basilica, the olive trees on the hill just behind the town, and seeing that none of our children got lost in the crowd. But when I got home and carefully reread his beautiful prayer, "Lord, Make Me an Instrument of Your Peace," I was profoundly moved.

After a lapse of 17 years, Mary Ann and I revisited Assisi in 1992. There we found the same majestic church, the same quiet crowds of tourists, the same narrow winding streets ascending the hill, and the same picturesque houses of soft pink and russet-colored stones. But I had changed. This time the good saint was uppermost in my mind and heart.

When we entered the lower church—almost dark, intimate, illuminated by candles—we went to the chapel of St. Francis, in a side alcove on the left, where we knelt in prayer. After finishing, we arose and turned to leave. On the way out I gave an offering for the shrine to a middle-aged, short, rather portly Franciscan brother, clothed in a rough brown habit. He spoke no English, and I spoke no Italian, but we understood each other. He gave me a card bearing the prayer that had come to mean so much to my patients and me, a prayer that had changed the lives of literally thousands of people in my acquaintance. As Mary Ann and I walked out in silence we knew that this had been a special moment in our lives.

Regardless of their creed, color or race, my patients took the spirit of this holy man with them when they left the hospital to continue their lives with a renewed sense of purpose. They took his words into their hearts and found great joy by living their lives for others. In like manner, this prayer has become a standard for me to live by, a means to restore and maintain my spiritual balance, and a guide to experience increased happiness in my life. My patients and I give these same words now to you.

Prayer of St. Francis

**Lord, make me an instrument
of your peace.**

Where there is hatred,
let me sow love;
Where there is injury, pardon;
Where there is doubt, faith;
Where there is despair, hope;
Where there is darkness, light;
And where there is sadness, joy.

O Divine Master, grant that I may not
so much seek to be consoled as to console;
to be understood as to understand;
to be loved as to love.

For it is in giving that we receive,
it is in pardoning that we are pardoned,
and it is in dying
that we are born to eternal life.

Need for Research

The Hope Heart Institute

Dr. Lester Sauvage founded The Hope Heart Institute in 1959 because at that time there was a pressing need to develop better operations and means with which to treat patients afflicted with heart and blood vessel diseases. During the next 20 years the Institute grew from a position of obscurity into one of international recognition as Dr. Sauvage and his staff made many important discoveries, including introduction of the coronary bypass operation using the patient's own veins (now the most common heart operation) and development of improved artificial grafts to replace or bypass diseased arteries.

In the early 1980s the Institute broadened its research scope to include prevention as well as treatment of heart disease. These new studies proved equally as successful as their surgical counterparts and both continue to be very productive today. During this same period the Institute developed a major educational mission for the lay public through creation of a monthly medical letter designed to help healthy people stay healthy. Today, four million people read this publication and millions more read other materials written by the Institute's educational staff under the direction of Carol Garzona.

The 1990s have thus far been a time of intense scientific excitement at the Institute as its talented and dedicated scientific staff have identified key research questions facing the field of cardiovascular disease and have accepted the challenge of contributing to their solutions. To aid in this effort, departments of Molecular Biology, Medical Engineering, and Clinical Research have been added to those established in earlier years—Chemistry and Hematology, Surgery, Cell Biology, Histology, and Vascular Healing.

The recent discovery by the Institute's staff that there is a healing cell in the blood which can convert the inner surface of an artificial blood vessel graft into a living natural structure is of the utmost importance. The Institute is fiercely committed to learning where this cell originates and determining how to control and extend its healing potential. Such basic scientific information could be of enormous biologic importance because it would advance understanding of how blood vessels heal and blood cells form, add knowledge that could help prevent hardening of the arteries (the problem that causes 96% of heart disease), and provide insight into how tumors develop a blood supply which enables them to grow and spread.

The Hope Heart Institute faces the oncoming millennium with optimism based on confidence arising from its many past accomplishments and on a passionate belief that heart disease can be defeated during our lifetimes if we all work together. In this all-out struggle for humankind, Dr. Sauvage as its Founder and Medical Director, views the work of the Institute as a means to serve God by serving humanity.

For more information about the Institute,
please call or write:

The Hope Heart Institute
556 18th Avenue
Seattle, WA 98122

Phone: (206) 328-8600   Fax: (206) 328-0355

About the Author

Dr. Lester Sauvage is a world-renowned heart surgeon, now retired, who has performed heart surgery for approximately 5,000 patients over 33 years, and for an equal number of patients requiring major blood vessel surgery. He pioneered the first experimental coronary bypass surgery using veins and the first use of the internal thoracic arteries to revascularize the entire human heart. Also, Dr. Sauvage pioneered the development of a line of artificial arteries, known as the Sauvage Graft, that are used worldwide. Certified by the American Board of Surgery and the American Board of Thoracic Surgery, he has also been awarded certificates for special competence in both pediatric and vascular surgery. Dr. Sauvage is a Clinical Professor of Surgery at the University of Washington School of Medicine.

Dr. Sauvage is the founder and medical director of The Hope Heart Institute, a leading institution in heart research. He has authored one medical book more than 225 scientific articles on heart and blood vessel surgery.

His many honors and awards include:

• Member, Alpha Omega Alpha Honorary Society, 1947

- Member, Alpha Sigma Nu Honor Society, 1948
- The degree HONORIS CAUSA, Seattle University, 1976
- The Vocational Service Award of the Rotary Club, 1977
- The Human Life Humanitarian Award, 1977
- The Brotherhood Award, National Conference of Christians and Jews, 1979
- The Clemson Award, Clemson University, for outstaning contributions in applied research in biomaterials, 1982
- The degree of Doctor of Science, Gonzaga University, 1982
- The Jefferson Award, American Institute for Public Service, 1983
- The Governor's Distinguished Volunteer Award, 1983
- The Spotlight Award, American Society of Women Accountants, 1985
- The Washington State Medal of Merit, 1987
- Honorary member of the New England Vascular Society
- First Citizen Award, Seattle-King County Association of Realtors, 1992
- Member, The American Surgical Association, 1995

Dr. Sauvage has a reputation for caring about people. He has been called "the Mother Teresa of heart surgery" because of the sacrificial care he provides for each and every patient, irrespective of their ability to pay, going beyond the call of duty to make sure their surgical experience was a positive and life-changing one. As Dr. C. Everett Koop, former Surgeon General of the United States, said, "Those who know him are impressed that undergirding all of the scientific accomplishments there is an ethic and morality that is lacking from the world of politics, business and even medicine today."

STORY BOOKS TO ENLIGHTEN AND ENTERTAIN

Catch the Whisper of the Wind
Inspirational Stories and Proverbs from Native Americans
Cheewa James

The richness of Native American culture is explored by noted motivational speaker and broadcast journalist Cheewa James. These provocative stories touch the heart and offer deep insight into the soul of the Indian.
Code 3693 . . . .**$11.95**

The 7th Floor Ain't Too High for Angels to Fly
A Collection of Stories on Relationships and Self-Understanding
John M. Eades, Ph.D.

In this diverse collection of provocative stories, therapist John Eades helps readers to reflect on how they are living their own lives and invites them to discover the inner resources that lead to true joy and fulfillment. You'll laugh and cry, but you won't be able to put down *The 7th Floor Ain't Too High for Angels to Fly.*
Code 3561 . . . .**$10.95**

Bedtime Stories for Grown-ups
Fairy-Tale Psychology
Sue Gallehugh, Ph.D. and Allen Gallehugh

In this witty, fully illustrated book, therapist Sue Gallehugh and her son Allen adapt classic fairy tales to illustrate the fundamental principles of self-love through mental health and psychological growth. This upbeat, entertaining book will leave readers laughing out loud as they explore the value of the serious concept of self-worth.
Code 3618 . . . .**$9.95**

Values from the Heartland
Bettie B. Youngs, Ph.D., Ed.D

One of the best-loved authors from *Chicken Soup for the Soul* shares uplifting, heartwarming tales, culled from her memories of growing up on a farm in Iowa. These value-laden stories will show you how hard times, when leavened with love and support, can provide strength of character, courage and leadership.
Code 3359: paperback **$11.95**
Code 3340: hard cover **$22.00**

Mentors, Masters and Mrs. MacGregor
Stories of Teachers Making a Difference
Jane Bluestein, Ph.D.

Jane Bluestein asked celebrities and common folks around the world the following question: Who is that one special teacher that made a difference in your life? The collected answers to this question make up this truly touching book which will appeal to the student—and the teacher—in all of us.
Code 3375: paperback **$11.95**
Code 3367: hard cover **$22.00**

Available at your favorite bookstore or call 1-800-441-5569 for Visa or MasterCard orders.
Prices do not include shipping and handling. Your response code is HCI.

Share the Magic of Chicken Soup

Chicken Soup for the Soul
101 Stories to Open the Heart and Rekindle the Spirit

The #1 *New York Times* bestseller and ABBY award-winning inspirational book that has touched the lives of millions.

Code 262X: Paperback $12.95
Code 2913: Hard cover $24.00
Code 3812: Large print $16.95

A 2nd Helping of Chicken Soup for the Soul
101 More Stories to Open the Heart and Rekindle the Spirit

This rare sequel accomplishes the impossible—it is as tasty as the original, and still fat-free.

Code 3316: Paperback $12.95
Code 3324: Hard cover $24.00
Code 3820: Large print $16.95

Chicken Soup for the Soul Cookbook
101 Stories with Recipes from the Heart

Here authors Jack Canfield, Mark Victor Hansen and award-winning cookbook author Diana von Welanetz Wentworth dish up a delightful collection of stories accompanied by mouthwatering recipes.

Code 3545: Paperback $16.95
Code 3634: Hard cover $29.95

A 3rd Serving of Chicken Soup for the Soul
101 More Stories to Open the Heart and Rekindle the Spirit

The latest addition to the *Chicken Soup for the Soul* series is guaranteed to put a smile in your heart.

Code 3790: Paperback $12.95
Code 3804: Hard cover $24.00

Available APRIL 1996

Available at your favorite bookstore or call
1-800-441-5569 for Visa or MasterCard orders. Prices do not include shipping and handling. Your response code is **HCI**.